ESTATE LIQUIDATION INS & OUTS:

WHAT TO DO WITH ANTIQUES AND MORE

BY

CONNIE MONAGHAN

Dedicated to the ladies who led the way:
Katie Monaghan, Mabel Long, and Eve Reynolds

And to my best friend, Frank Vos

*Additional thanks to Sue McFadden, Mike and Colleen at Accent on Antiques,
Cassandra, and a variety of antique professionals, customers, and friends who
would most likely prefer to remain unnamed*

The author's blog, "Antiques in the Modern World," can be
found at conniemonaghan.com. Her Facebook site is
Antiques a Go Go.

On the cover: a folk art, wrought-iron candelabra, approximately 3 feet high, maker
and age unknown

TABLE OF CONTENTS

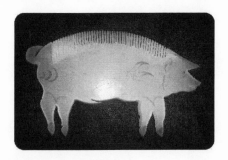

CHAPTER 1: IS THIS BOOK FOR YOU?

There are lots of books out there on how to sell antiques for fun 'n' profit. This isn't one of them. This is for you, the poor gal weeping into her bowl of Cheerios that there's just no way to handle all the stuff you've inherited. There's no time, there's no space, and it's too painful to think about! Or for you, the woman who's cool, organized... and absolutely unprepared to help Dad downsize and move into a retirement home. Dad himself may be curious about all the things he still has in boxes... inherited from his own dad 30 years ago! And secretly you're wondering... what would happen if it all mysteriously went over Niagara Falls?

The information here will help you to know: whether your things are antique, vintage, retro or other; how to find the value of your items; and the various ways you can liquidate that one little vase or an entire mansionful: should you keep, sell, donate... or throw those estate items over Niagara Falls?

In these pages you'll find detailed information on how estate services companies and auction houses work and whether they might be useful to you. You'll learn how to sell to antique stores and at antique sales and flea markets. The wide variety of selling options, from a homegrown garage sale to a high-end auction, are explained in detail. You'll learn what each method of selling entails, what its costs and benefits are, and how to choose the method – or combination of methods – best for you.

You'll learn how to sort and value your own items, what professional appraisers do, and about the many resources that can help you in your selling. Is this book for you? See if any of these scenarios ring a bell:

◆ When your mother/father/grandma passed on, you became responsible for a houseful of cherished (and not-so-cherished) stuff, including a lot of items that might have value... you're just not sure. Overwhelming? Hey, yes! There are things that you love, but you can't keep it all. After the family has taken what it wants, what on earth do you do with the rest?

◆ You and your husband, retired and loving it, are hitting the road on your matching Harleys – and your new tattoo reads, "Born to Get Rid of Junk." But how? There's the family fort – four bedrooms, attic, and basement – to contend with. All those memory-laden mementos, from your son's high school trophies to your huge collection of cookbooks – are such a burden! Should you just call Salvation Army and be done with it?

◆ You're a happy clutterbug (like me) with way too much of everything. It's all swell but... *It's Alive!* .... and it's taken over every drawer, closet, table top... even the empty fireplace! You'd love to turn your old sewing room into.... well, back into a sewing room, but how to sort out the good stuff from the not-so-great? That Pet Rock from 1975... it's practically ancient and pretty neato... but is it valuable? (And will selling it solve the problem?)

◆ Money money money money money money money.... you sure could use some! And what's the use of all your long-gone dad's collectibles taking up room in the garage when you could sell them and pay down the Visa card? You haven't opened those boxes in years, and don't even know what's in them... books? Old toys? Whatever's there, it's time for it to go!

◆ Marriage/divorce brought you together/tore you apart, and now there's no need for two of everything. Out with... what? Is there an easy way to make some money by selling off the extra stuff?

◆ Your mother-in-law gave you a "lovely" clown painting that she says is valuable. Is it? Is there any way to get it out of your house without crushing her?! It's too big to hide behind the potted plant in your living room. Re-gift it to a frenemy? *Hmmm...*

Each situation has its own vexing challenges. If you're dealing with a houseful of things, you'll probably have a wide variety of the good, the bad, the desirable, and the worthless. Keep reading to learn how to separate the wheat from the chaff... and to find out whether you even want to get that far in the process. If the whole shebang is just too much, jump to "Chapter 14: Estate Services" to find out how to dispose of all those worldly goods in the easiest manner possible.

As for myself, my mother passed on a few years ago, leaving my dad with a large house that held the accumulation of 50 years of marriage, three kids, and two grandchildren. His response was apparently typical of older men (I've heard similar stories from numerous friends): he wanted everything gone instantly and he didn't care how it happened! He literally couldn't face the treasures and junk that had made up their life together. I'd like to believe it was too painful for him, but who knows – at his age, maybe he just needed to move on as quickly as possible. A mere four months later the house was emptied and sold and he was remarried to a high school pal from 60-odd years ago!

In the meantime, my sister and I were in a panic. We both lived hours away, and didn't even know the half of what was in the house. From basement to attic, we spent weekends looking through things in order to save family history and .... And what?! We weren't even sure why we were taking the time to do it; it just had to be done

It's no surprise that in hindsight we did everything wrong. I felt that the curtain had suddenly closed on the theater of my life in that house. The leading lady was gone, the show was over, and I could see no reason to keep the props. And so we invited friends to help themselves to things they wanted. We threw together an utterly disorganized estate sale in a week's time and sold things ridiculously cheaply and with little thought as to the future. Though I'd been casually buying and selling antiques since high school, I wasn't aware of the choices we had. I didn't know there were whole-estate buyers, or auctions geared toward selling average household goods. It didn't occur to me to save some of the better things in storage until we'd have a clearer perspective on our options. In the grip of grief it's easy to make mistakes, thinking that all is lost. (And dealing with relatives can truly muddy the waters.)

My mantra at the time was "You can't keep everything." My mantra looking back is, "There's no sense in looking back; you can't blame yourself." We did our best, and everything disappeared one way or another. I have a few things that I'm happy that I kept but regrets that I didn't keep others. That's life, really, though, isn't it? And certainly in the antiques world, regrets are par for the course. The *should*s and *could've*s can drive you crazy. But armed with information, and a little time to consider your options, the regrets recede in the face of smarter choices.

In the hopes of entertaining the reader while illustrating points about selling things, I've interspersed a number of "Adventures in the Junk Trade" true stories from The Cat's Pajamas Antiques. Names have been changed to protect the peculiar and the guilty!

Adventures in the Junk Trade: From Way Upriver

My little antique store is a block off Main Street, not far from the Columbia River, in Vancouver, Washington. If you happen to exit the freeway here rather than drive south for another 10 minutes to Portland, or a few hours north to Seattle, you'll find The Cat's Pajamas on a tree-lined side street downtown. In the late 1950s, Willie Nelson hosted a radio show from KVAN on lower Main. Meanwhile, 15 blocks up at the north end of Main, teens hung out at the Dairy Queen, which is still there. They "cruised the gut," the long-ago pastime of driving slowly up Main, around the DQ, and back down Broadway to do it all over again while listening to Willie on the radio and flirting out the window.

Eventually, when outlying malls took root and the downtown went to seed as it did in so many small towns, you could still hear Willy singing "Blue Skies" from one card room jukebox or another down there, year after year.

To the city's credit, downtown Vancouver's been remarkably revitalized. From the DQ on down Main there are shops and restaurants; the once-sad park hosts a bandstand now, and a terrific farmer's market; a new library was built to take advantage of the vast view across the river... still, the pleasant square mile or so carries remnants of its tougher past: pawn shops, bail bond offices, and the county jail, all of which lead to an occasionally interesting *clientele.*

The first time their rattle-trap truck pulled up, I could tell, watching from behind my counter, that he'd come from a-way up river like Martin Sheen in Apocalypse Now. *As he stepped into the daylight, the grit in his eye said he'd seen things there he'd never forget: the horror. The horror. Either that, or the nine motherless pit bull puppies currently squirming blindly on his couch (as his wife later described). His shirt was greasy; it flapped over a rising-dough stomach; and the rasp in his voice reflected that long, taxing journey through the jungle of junk – the arrows slung at him from unseen hands, the Goodwill clerks who just* Didn't. Effing. Care! *There were standards in this world. He wasn't sure what they were, but having to pay the* Goddam Vet *even after the mother dog died was... well, they couldn't afford it, that's all. So him and Claudine had left their double-wide upriver after piling the truck bed with a lotta stuff – treasures they'd been saving for a store they wanted to open sometime, somewhere – and here they were at the Cat's Antiques. They had actually meant to go a few more blocks to that better-known antique store, but then decided that the owner was too snooty for them. Plus, they were low on gas. So here they were. Did I want some Beatles lunchboxes? Repops, true, but the Yellow Submarine snow globe was going for at least 85 on Ebay.*

Long-story-short, Claudine and Juggler turned out to be likable people who just had a lotta trouble in their lives besides the pit bull, besides the trailer that burnt down, besides their son in prison. It was just like that – one trouble led to another; for instance when the truck broke down and Claudine called Juggler to come help and they got into a shouting match on the side of the road but he never touched her; still someone called the sheriff and he went to jail for domestic violence and then, and then, and then.... but that was later, the low point of the whole string of trouble, like one Christmas light bulb popping out after the other and pretty soon the tree's on fire and they're sitting there with smoking hair wondering what happened. But that was later.

Before that, over several months, the pair of them brought in gunny sacks of junk. On any particular day they might've been scrapping metal, hauling busted bicycles, bed springs, washers from their burg up the winding highway along the Columbia, an hour away. They were usually smeared with dirt and rust, their goods reeking of the fertile mud that coated them. It always took a long time to go through the stuff as Claudine spun out the stories and peeled off layers of resentment: the parole officer who wouldn't listen, the neighbor who threatened to shoot them for one thing and another; as much as I'd later complain to myself as I scraped dirt off a toy, I never seriously considered asking them not to come back. In a world of bland they were hardscrabble authentic, interesting to listen to, and most vividly alive. It was the struggle that kept them kicking. I liked Claudine especially, her toughness, and the tough love that bound her to Juggler. And they had a good eye for the junk: a four-foot-tall Nehi sign, a vintage WWII glass tank, Victorian doorknobs...

The last time I saw Claudine, Juggler had gotten two years in jail for what she said was his sham arrest on the word of the witness/liar who'd called in the roadside "assault." Unlucky for her she'd blown a tire the morning of his trial and wasn't able to testify. She didn't have much to sell me: a couple of bottles she'd dug (and had the dirty fingernails to prove it), a pair of candlesticks. I didn't need them and couldn't sell them, but I bought them out of loyalty and the knowledge that I could easily be in her shoes... but if I were, I couldn't have worn them with such chutzpah, ingenuity, tenacity. Claudine was a good one. I wished her luck and waved as her truck rattled off.

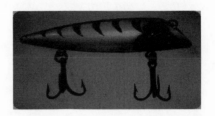

CHAPTER 2: PLANNING AHEAD AS YOU READ THE BOOK

In the museum world, one does not "get rid of junk"! Neither does a museum have a fire sale, a blow-out, or a rummage-o-rama in order to raise cash. Instead, should the museum's storerooms and warehouses become overstuffed with valuable art and artifacts; or should the museum be in need of funds (one never says *cash, moola,* or *dough-di-o-dough* when referring to the institution's money), the museum simply *deaccessions* a painting or dinosaur bone or Warhol soup can from its inventory.

You, too, can deaccession your valuable possessions, whether woeful prints of big-eyed children or Henry the VIII's sterling serving pieces. And should your pesky in-laws ask, "Whatever happened to that lovely painting we gave you of the clown smoking a stogie?" just shrug vaguely, smile kindly, and say, "Oh, it was just so wonderful that we deaccessioned it, thanks for asking!" They'll never guess.

> From Merriam-Webster Dictionary, the definition of *deaccession*: "To sell or otherwise dispose of (an item in the collection) <the museum deaccessioned several paintings>

Advice on sorting out an estate is located toward the end of the book (see "Part III"), with the belief that learning about the selling options first will help you make more informed decisions about particular items or groups of things. As you read through the book, what looks to you now like an incomprehensible and overwhelming mess may clarify into various categories, such as "send to auction," "garage sale," and "donate." In order to ease your own way, at this point it'll be helpful to make a list of things that you already know you want to deaccession, such as:

Mother's good china

Player piano

Uncle Chuck's 78 records

Ruby glass collection

Lionel train set

Scrapbook of old valentines

Pyrex bowls & casseroles

Washer/dryer

Take notes as you go, such as "Trains: collector clubs, ask at antique mall"; "washer: local auction house," "jewelry: find appraiser."

<u>Overview of Selling Options</u>

Not including arson (!), there are really only three ways to purposely deaccession things: give them away, sell them, or throw them out. The various ways of selling that we'll look at are: garage sales; auctions, both high- and low-end; selling to antique stores; estate services; antique shows and flea markets; Ebay and Craigslist. You'll learn how each choice might work for you (or not), including specific costs and benefits, and what to be careful of.

CHAPTER 3: WHAT'S IT WORTH?

Adventures in the Junk Trade: Hidden Money

Let's say on Valentine's Day, Juan Derful gifts you with a tackle box of crusty fishing stuff. There's a tangle of lines, a couple old-fashioned reels, rusty-barbed lures, plus one of those corny fishing baskets. Meanwhile, Mr. E. Mann gives you a set of his grandmother's lovely old Depression glass plates. There are a couple of tiny chips, but they're nothing really, and the soft pink matches your poodle's dye job. Which generous suitor should you be extra thankful to? And which of these paramours should go swim with the fishes?

An older gal we'll call Shelly invited my boyfriend/partner Frank and I to her house last year to buy a few things from her collection of "valuable antiques." Imagine our mounting excitement when, after taking us on a tour of the incredible Art Nouveau statues and stained glass in her living room, she led us out to a cluttered garage (the best kind!) to see the boxes she told us were "just for us"! Wow! Never mind the winter shivers we instantly shook with. This might be a sweet deal! She was getting rid of treasured things, great things, incredible things! (Picture me, a walking cliche, rubbing my greedy little paws together out as I dance from foot to foot in gleeful anticipation!)

As she pulled the first tattered box up onto the ironing board you might've thought I was Super Picker, staring hard at the cardboard to see through it to the goodies inside. But.... rats! It didn't take much sleuthing to see that these super-special treats were in boxes marked "Garage Sale" – a sale she admitted she'd already had! Wonderful!, I groaned silently. The dregs! Well, we were there, so we patiently nodded and shivered and "mm hmm"ed through a parade of hideous vases, ho-hum plates, and an ugly "modern" statue circa 1984. All of this and to have our tootsies frozen off simultaneously? Dang!

After showing us a tableful of such things while I politely repeated, "Sorry, not for me," she brought out a small lozenge tin with mother-of-pearl wafers inside it that she vaguely remembered her mother-in-law had said were some sort of Chinese dealies that could be made into jewelry. Okay, whatever. I was getting hungry and losing my composure. They were interesting but most likely fairly useless, and I put them in the "keep" pile just to say I'd bought something.

When she got to the fishing gear her husband left behind when he went to the Great Fishing Hole in the Sky I could see that the old woven fishing baskets (I didn't know they were called creels) had an appealing decorative look. One of my customers liked maritime collectibles, and I figured that a creel might do. I ended up forking over 50 hard-earned bucks for two creels, an old tackle box holding a few crusty lures, and the Chinese thingies. We begged off on the rest, which disappointed her greatly, and off we schlepped, into the winter blues.

"So, whattya think, Frank?" I asked as we settled into the car to leave. He shrugged ever deeper into his puffy jacket and gazed through the frosted windshield. Not a good sign.

"Geez, I had to buy something from her," I said. "She was so insistent."

"Yeah," he muttered, "but I think you overpaid for it."

Well, I sold the creels relatively cheaply at $35 each, and when I put the first lure on Ebay at $1.99, to my surprise it immediately generated a *lot of attention. After a Texas lure dealer contacted me, I learned the good way that old wooden lures with glass eyes can be worth quite a lot, sometimes in the hundreds of dollars. And yep, the Chinese mother-of-pearl chips, no bigger than postage stamps, turned out to be 100-year-old gambling tokens worth $10-$25 apiece.*

It was never my intention to the get the best of the lure lady. A good deal, for me, means that we both end up satisfied. Unfortunately for her, she had no idea what her fishing gear was worth, or what the mother-of-pearl squares were, and neither did I. I took a risk that I could make my money back; she took the risk that every antique dealer knows the value of everything ever made in every era, ever. Ahem! They don't. On the other hand, she was quite happy with what she got, just disappointed that we hadn't bought more.

As I write this, in the two-thousand-teens, there's distinct generation gap in the use of technology: many of my older customers don't use – or want to use – computers. Had this lady done a quick check on Ebay, she would have found equivalent values for her lures and gambling pieces. If, for whatever reason, you don't use a computer, ask someone who does to give you a little help so that you can get a ballpark value of your items. It's important and could cost you more than you imagine!

(By the way, the Depression glass given by Mr. E. Mann is worth very little in its chipped condition.)

The question "What's it worth?" is at the crux of every deal, and every time you buy or sell you most likely question whether you're paying too much or asking too little. "What's it worth?" will be a constant wonder as you look through items you're not sure about.

I used to think there was an absolute *worth* for every item, a worth that didn't change, wasn't negotiable, and was written in stone (somewhere, by someone!) This belief was validated by the zillions of price guides that give worth values for almost any item you can imagine, in every collecting category. A Little Red Riding Hood cookie jar, for example, was worth exactly $125.99 in 1993, no more, no less. Eezy-peezy! No sweat. The problem was, when I had my first antique-mall booth, I couldn't get that amount no matter what I did! Nobody would pay it, and this was in Los Angeles! I just couldn't understand what the problem was. (Never mind that the mall was in a high tourist area where folks didn't want to buy cookie jars to haul home to Tennessee.) I finally surrendered, lowered the price, and sold it – a decent lesson in marketplace economics that I've since learned time and time again: the market dictates the price, not the other way around.

Twenty years later we're in a recession, my store is off the beaten track in a fairly small town… and you can toss the price guide out the window! If my customer only has twenty bucks of fun money this week, he's not going to spend $19 of it on a doodad that he perceives to be overpriced, no matter what the book says it's worth. (If 10 customers look at that fishing reel but pass it up, I know I have it priced wrong.)

When deciding what you want for your things, there are better questions to ask than "What's it worth?"

- What's an approximate value on the marketplace today? (See "Chapter 7: Getting a Clue")

- How much would you like to get for it? (If you're going to feel badly getting only, say, $20, then make sure you price it higher)

- What's it worth to you to be rid of it? Five dollars? Twenty? If your goal is simply to liquidate an estate, will you be happy enough just to have it gone and to have a little extra change in your pocket?

- How much would you pay for it in a store? At an auction?

These are questions that guide a variety of values that can be placed on any one item. Let's say Grandma left Darcy a beautiful Japanese vase. Darcy adores it, but with two little kids in the house, she's worried it'll get broken if she displays it. Also, Darcy knows the vase is an antique and might be worth quite a bit, and man, do those diaper costs add up!

Should she sell it?, she wonders. Here are the different ways to consider the value of any item, just as Darcy will think about her vase:

Retail value: This is what a merchant might price it at in a store. Let's say the merchant puts $200 on it. (This is not, however, what you would get for it if you sold it. See "Chapter 8: You Can't Make Money Without Spending Some".)

Auction or fair-market value: To determine this, an appraiser will look up comparable sales results. What have vases such as this one generally sold for at other auctions? Auction value is generally less than retail value by a third or so. Darcy's vase might sell for $100 at auction.

Insurance value: This is what the appraiser decides it would cost the insurance company to replace it in case of damage or theft. This is usually well above retail value by a third, so the appraiser may put an insurance value on the same vase for $300.

There are a couple of other considerations that aren't talked about when deciding the value of an item. The first, and possibly biggest influence on how dear you hold something is the sentimental value. It might just kill Darcy to sell that vase for even a penny under what she believes it's worth. Fair enough. It belongs to her, and it matters greatly to her, so it's important that she choose her market carefully (if at all). Folks occasionally bring things into my store to sell, then waffle when it comes time to actually hand the item over. Sometimes a higher offer on my part will do the trick, but I often just tell them, "Don't sell it if it's gonna hurt too much! Don't sell it if you're going to regret it."

Last is what I'll call Relief or Grief Value: Will you be relieved or distressed that it's gone? For Darcy, it'll be Grief as she'll miss the vase and wish she'd kept it. If the vase happened to be one that your mean old stepmother left you – a grotesque reminder of unhappy times – the relief value in getting rid of it might be so great that you won't mind selling it cheaply just so you don't have to think about it again.

I've heard other answers to the question "What's it worth?" The most accurate, probably, is "It's worth what you can get for it." While this might seem flip, it's also maddeningly true. A better answer is "It's worth what the market will bear." Both of these beg the questions of "Which market?" and "Can I get more for it at a summer auction in Poughkeepsie?"

CHAPTER 4: ANTIQUE, VINTAGE, RETRO... WHAT'S THE DIFFERENCE?

What's an antique? What's the difference between vintage and retro? And: Is an ancient dust bunny a collectible? If not, why not?

Adventures in the Junk Trade: Oh, the Humanity!

In the last week I've had several encounters with – let's use the made-up word "unknowledgeable" – women who wanted to sell me things. They were neither stupid nor uneducated, simply lacking knowledge about antiques. The first called the store to ask whether I'd be interested in buying her grandmother's homemade quilts. "Are they old?" I asked. "Oh yes, very old!" Visions of hand-quilted Texas Star masterpieces danced in my head.

"In good condition?" The answer was yes. I couldn't wait! Twenty minutes later a tall young gal presented herself at my counter, her arms loaded with... crocheted acrylic-yarn throws and a garish-looking polyester thing in blocks of primary colors. It all reeked of cigarette smoke. I picked through it all briefly, smiled, apologized, and pointed out the poorly embroidered signature and date. "I'm sorry, but it's just not old enough," I said.

She was shocked!, shocked that this incredible relic from way back in 1983 wasn't in the Smithsonian, really, with the dinosaur bones, I suppose. She actually gasped. "All I want is fifty dollars!" I gave her a tolerant yet painful grin, raised my eyebrows, and sweetly whispered, "Me too."

Not long afterward, an older lady trotted through my door like a spring lamb, a large picture frame in hand. "I see you've brought me a painting," I said, flaunting the results of many years of higher education.

She smiled, eyes wide with excitement, and turned the frame around to show off ... a crafty cut-yarn coat-of-arms thingie circa 1973. In burnt orange and harvest gold. In an avocado-green frame. Naturally! "Gubbers," it read under the shield.

"My my!" I muttered enthusiastically, truly at a loss for words.

She was a Gubbers and couldn't understand why none of the plethora of Gubbers offspring wanted it, she explained in exasperation. "I even wrote the whole story of it down," she said. "I just don't get it!"

"Might be the mildew spots," I suggested blandly. She blinked, awaiting a big appraisal. "The name," I continued in my smarty-pants-antique-dealer vein, "might make it difficult to sell."

"But there are lots of Gubbers!"

"I'm sorry, it's just not for me," I said.

She was heartbroken. She truly was. "Are you sure you don't want it?!" She lingered like a schoolgirl hoping to get noticed; hoping I'd see the light of the beautiful thing she'd made with love so many years ago. I felt for her just as I'd felt for the LOL (little old lady, like me) who sold me her handmade tablecloth in order to pay the rent. I didn't want it but I bought it just the same. And over the years there've been too many people to count who "just need a little money for gas" or to bail Junior out of jail or to simply buy a bag of groceries. I'm pretty sure I'll be standing right behind them before long so I try to give them kindness if not that $50 they're looking for.

"Just because it's not right for me doesn't mean someone else won't love it," I offered lamely. She left the store no longer a lamb but a sad old dog dragging its tail in the dirt. It's just not fun to see folks' dreams crushed...

It's not surprising that most people know little about antiques. Why should they? But if you plan to sell your things, it will pay off handily to know what you have... and what you don't have.

One thing to note is that neither of these women had ever been in my store before, and probably hadn't been in any antique store in years. They were utterly unfamiliar with the market, let alone with the goods in my shop. So Step One – should you decided to take on the mission of educating yourself about antiques in general – should be to visit a number of antique stores and malls, hang around Ebay, watch the many collector and pawn shop TV shows (more on them later, but they do educate in palatable dollops), and check out the many books on any specialized area you want to know more about. You'll be surprised at how much info you can glean.

First Things First: Is it Antique?

It's time to look at each item on the "sell" list you made at the beginning. You'll want to do your own assessment on it for a first guess as to: Is it antique? Something else? Is it appropriate to the antiques market?

But hey, what the heck does *antique* really mean? The definition varies, but generally 75 to 100 years old. That said, most antique stores (except the snotty high-end ones filled with curly gold French metal stuff and whale's teeth carved by OCD sailors of yore) aren't full of antiques, which are generally crazy-expensive, fragile and in many cases, truly unwanted anymore except by those who live in piles of stone on Park Avenue. Or in France, of course. (Kraut cutter, anyone? Spinning wheel? Thousand-dollar teapot?) The olden days were full of big wooden things that no one has room for anymore, and breakable items that no one can afford.

It's more likely that your local antique mall is stuffed with *vintage* items: from 25 to 75 years old, often fitting into a category such as Mid-century Modern, Art Deco, or 1950s kitchenware. *Vintage* can cover a wide range of tastes, from low end to high. A shag carpet from the '70s is vintage, as is a beautiful, valuable diamond necklace from the 1950s.

Retro is a term used loosely for either actual vintage items or more often for reproductions of vintage items. There are brand-new retro diners that look like the places from the 1950s. You'll find retro décor even in large department stores in nearly every category of item now, from retro watches to retro bar ware. It may have that vintage look but it's new and has the price tag to match. When sorting through items looking for authentic older pieces, beware of bar codes, "Made in China" labels, or any item that just looks too shiny-new to be true. It may be retro, but it's probably too recently made to be considered collectible.

Shabby chic, in some corners of the antiques world, has become a shabby code phrase for both *fakey French* and *Made in China* décor. Once a smart decorator's idea of re-creating, say, the charm of a rich family's Nantucket beach house – one that's been visited by generations over dozens of years, complete with worn chintz, slipcovers and chipped-up white furniture (think the Kennedy clan) – it's mutated into a strange business of sanding the corners off perfectly good tables, ruining lovely wood pieces with chalkboard paint, and putting ribbons around Mason jars full of sea shells... sea shells purchased by the boxful from China! Loads of imitation shabby chic items fill the aisles of discount stores, from weathered seagull plaques to "Believe" signs. (Nope, I never understood those, either!) It's all a matter of personal taste, but if the items you want to sell fall into this category, they may not be old at all.

Collectibles can describe anything from yesterday's McDonald's Happy Meal toy to Mickey Mantle's glove to a Disney animation cel from the 1930s. Collectibles generally fall into specific categories, such as autographs, yo-yos, firecracker labels, Corgi cars, Hallmark Christmas ornaments, movie memorabilia, baseball cards, etc. Collectibles can be brand-new or antique. If you're dealing with a big collection of any one thing (oh dear, late Aunt May collected *how many* Schlitz beer signs?) it falls into this category. (Please note: anything that was marketed as a collectible, such as Bradford Exchange plates, Franklin Mint items, etc., is unlikely to actually be collectible.) Various areas of collectibles, such as Hummel figures, Lladro, and Barbies have dropped drastically in value. (See "Chapter 6: The Changing Marketplace.")

Pop culture collectibles refers to what's happening now in music, TV, cartoons, etc. My nieces are into anime, manga and other Japanese pop culture trends that I haven't a clue about. There are also *vintage* pop culture collectibles, like a lunch box featuring the Beatles, or a Fred Flintstone paper tablecloth.

For the purposes of this book all vintage, collectibles, and actual antiques will be referred to as... antique (now is that confusing, or what?!).

Adventures in the Junk Trade: All the World's a Stage

Adam's a regular, a mild, friendly guy who designs bicycles for a living. He looks like a grownup slacker, like a guy who's never worn a tie and may occasionally eat Spaghetti-Os and beer for dinner; he has a bunch of little kids and escapes it all, apparently, by repurchasing the good times of his own childhood years: a Bugs Bunny Halloween mask, Batman toys, and, a couple of months ago, a James Bond movie poster: Live or Let Die. *He doesn't collect anything in particular, he says. He's purchased 1950s Halloween decorations, a raggedy Barbie doll, a Charlie Chaplin pencil box...*

Yesterday at lunchtime he ambled in, hands in pants pockets, as laid back as ever. "Do you have any more movie posters?" he asked. "Like the one I bought before?" As it happened, I had bought another Bond poster recently but had already traded it to another dealer.

"So sorry," I shrugged. "The best I can do is a one-armed Shirley Temple paper doll."

He wandered around, settling on a Mad Magazine Spy Vs. Spy *paperback that I'd bought from a blonde gal I'll call Carrie who said she was downsizing, just getting rid of stuff. I hear that a lot and don't think twice as I've done it myself with carloads of too much.*

"Any more of these?" he asked, hefting the book. I thought a minute and checked my pile of disorganized merchandise that had yet to be priced.

"Just this one." I pulled out a Mad: The Lighter Side. *He nodded and smiled. "It's in pretty sad shape," I said, "so I can sell it cheap."*

He nodded again and paid for the books, barely acknowledging my efforts at smalltalk. As I handed him his change, he flipped to the inside back cover of the second book and pointed to a devil drawn in crayon.

"My son Alda drew that," he said. I didn't understand. "My ex-wife stole these from me, and the movie poster, too."

As it dawned on me – Ohhhhhh... damn! – I even recalled her name: Carrie. A casual blonde, cool as a cuke, losing her high school prettiness but well dressed. Jeez, I felt just terrible!

"I just won't buy anything from her again!" I told him, feeling a confused personal outrage. I thought I should do something drastic, but he seemed wryly nonplussed.

"I wouldn't worry about it," he said, heading for the door. "I don't think she'll do it again."

The moral of the story? While the things of the antique world may be interesting objects, they're merely props to the fascinating human dramas they play a part in!

CHAPTER 5: IS IT SELLABLE?

Believe it or not, there are only three reasons that people buy something, old or new: it's useful, it's decorative, or it's collectible. If it's none of those, then it's useless in every regard, and the buyer will pass. Looking at your one item or even your entire estate from the perspective of the buyer, then, it might be easier than you think to sort out the sellable from the not-so-much – whether you know anything about antiques or not.

Useful is the trickiest category as it can mean a number of things, including useful for nostalgia, status, and investment. A vintage mixing bowl can be useful in the practical sense, but it's also useful in holding memories of mom (or grandma) in her 1950s kitchen. A sterling candelabra can be useful on the table, but also useful in conveying status and as an investment (for someone gambling that either the price of silver or the value of the antique will go up). Even a torn old road map can be found useful by a crafty person for making decoupage.

Because of the variety of ways in which an item might be useful to a buyer, you won't always be able to guess if it falls into this category (who knew that the torn baseball jersey would be grabbed up by your neighbor nostalgic for her old team?) but in general if it's broken, the last remaining silver-plated fork in a set, heavily used (no one wants old Tupperware!), or way out of fashion (dad's mullet toupee?!), put it in either the "donate" or "dump" category. If the jersey happened to belong to Babe Ruth? Time to book that ticket to the Caribbean, as it would be a hugely desirable collectible!

Collectible Don't toss anything before an expert takes a look! (Even the above.) The "#$*!!&* junk" your late husband amassed in the garage may have more value than you think; your daughter's Cabbage Patch doll might be desirable; even the stack of old TV Guides that grandma stuck away in the cellar has value. Lots of things that you think are useless may be collectible, such as ticket stubs, pens & stationery, family photos, vintage curtains and fabrics, letters and other paper goods, bottles and tins. I often find collectible coffee cans overlooked – even at estate sales – because they're out in the garage holding nails. I've found terrific primitives, such as cupboards, benches, and stools utterly unnoticed by those selling the household goods. There are neat things to be found outside, too, such as cement statuary, vintage patio furniture, and pottery flower pots. There are collectors of game pieces (you don't need the complete game), kids Halloween costumes, brass hose nozzles, airline barf bags, pipes, harmonicas, ...

One of my better estate finds was an umbrella, probably from the 1950s or early '60s, priced at $7. The plaid rayon wasn't in perfect shape but it was charming nonetheless... I thought. No one else thought so, though, and it sat in my crock o' canes for more than a year. I hauled it to antique shows and flea markets with no luck! Dealers came and went, hungry for any item to make a buck on, but they showed no interest at all. Finally, at loose ends one day, I tested the red handle for Bakelite (the plastic popular from the 1940s-1960s, used for jewelry, knobs, and industrial parts), and bingo! I sold it on Ebay for more than $300! While Bakelite jewelry has taken a dive, chunky pieces and certain colors are going for a fortune in Europe... another mystery of the antiques market. I know it sounds nuts, but it just goes to the point that surprising things can be valuable, despite all odds!

Decorative As trends shift, last year's junk becomes becomes this year's must-have loft décor, such as rusty scrap and steampunky nonworking clocks. In a major city, being "on-trend" means literally the latest thing. In smaller towns such as mine, though, these tastes have yet to hit the shore. I enjoy Asian antiques and Victorian clutter while my live-in boyfriend prefers stark Mid-century Modern. You'll still find plenty of Colonial Kitsch and '70s shag among the local homes (as well as Asian Mid-century Victorian Nightmare!). (It's also true that a good friend here keeps the curtains pulled on her 1920s house in order to hide the actual stuffed lion, calf, birds, monkey... even her beloved taxidermied pit bull... arrayed among the Gothic furniture, a Victrola, and, cobwebbed chandeliers.)

Thus, the market for décor is all over the place: again, don't throw anything out! The paint-by-numbers you did as a child are considered the heighth of hip by lots of young people, and in my shop I sell old cameras, trophies, and telephones as décor.

As with all categories, the exception to the "don't-throw-out" rule is anything that's in extremely poor condition. And then there are the exceptions to the exception: Besides rusty metal and industrial decay, an example of good-bad condition would be yard art. That concrete burro will actually look better given some moss, outdoor aging, and a chipped ear!

Adventures in the Junk Trade: Useless!

Earlier today, as I was attempting to organize the sea of stuff that regularly floats onto my counter – an antique medical bill, pens that work and don't, a gold chain with a pendant holding gold flakes, cement squirrel, ballpeen hammer, paper clips, jewelry tags, loose marbles – a man in his late 30s pulled his bike up outside, shoving my blue baby buggy full of chrysanthemums out of the way to park it. Dark hair, black windbreaker, he was all business as he stepped in, set his backpack on my counter and opened a zipper to take out a small metal compact, acting as if it were all in a day's work to show me his wares, though I'd never laid on eyes on him before.

He barely returned my hello, and I didn't feel particularly chatty, considering the flower abuse. He might've been a mysterious movie character – a secret agent, maybe – as he demonstrated the attributes of the little box. First, holding it high on his palm, he flipped open the lid. Then, using his thumbnail, he opened the inner compartment. I was expecting powder. He took a moment, as a magician would: Behold! I looked, and looked again. There they were: two glass discs, each resting in a shallow depression. If I'd been drinking coffee I would've done a spit take.

"They're contacts!" I sputtered. He took a breath and looked, gazing with his own kind of awe. "Yeah... but they're old!"

"Uh..." I'd met clueless before, but this one left me speechless. "Not. Uh... sorry."

And with that, he was out the door again and peddling away like the Wicked Warlock of the West.

There's no moral to this story, except: not every treasure is a treasure, and don't run over the flowers!

CHAPTER 6: THE CHANGING MARKETPLACE

Ladies in their 60s often wander wistfully through the store, ruminating on all the dishes, linens, and glass they own but don't want anymore. They secretly hope I'll offer to take it off their hands for big bucks. Instead, I kindly suggest they send their cast-offs to China, where poor children don't have nice sets of Noritake and shelves full of Fenton silvercrest ruffled-edge bowls. Why would I even joke about such thing? Because Americans are rich in *stuff* that no one really needs. And young people don't want these things. It's rough to hear it. The ladies sigh. I explain that it's the times, the change in tastes, the recession... I hate to tell them, but the ground that the antiques trade rests on has shifted dramatically. Boomers aren't buying anymore. Younger folks don't have the same outlook and aren't looking for what the older generation has enjoyed.

Oh, well, they remark sweetly... *it all comes back around.* They're unwilling to hear that much of what's now out of fashion in the antiques world is likely permanently out of fashion. Will the baby names Doris, Mildred, and Dorothy ever be as popular as they were in the 1930s? Someone will always be named John, Bill, or Mary – of course, they're classics – but trends change for good. The world moves on.

Still, the thought that one day their treasures will hot again style satisfies them that their collecting days weren't for naught, that all that money and passion spent on Roseville and Westmoreland and red-handled kitchen gadgets and Bauer bowls and Pyrex sets and Shawnee vases and

McCoy wishing wells and Early American pressed glass and Santa Anita Ware and –

No, I might say, feeling deeply cruel, *it's never coming back around.*

Mrs. Whoever then smarts as if I'd slapped her. She doesn't want to hear that the younger generation has about as much interest in Vaseline glass as she herself had in buggy whips and spats; that is to say, none!

<u>Can antiques be counted on to go up in value, year in and year out? And if not, why not?</u>

The selling market, like the stock market, is an up-and-down affair, often surprising, occasionally deeply depressing or wildly exhilarating... but always, *always* changing. What's popular today might be passe next year. Or tomorrow! To paraphrase Heidi Klum, "One day it's in, and then it's out." Knowing what's selling and what's not may flabbergast, astonish, and astound you – "You mean my husband's father's chalkware collection isn't worth a tinker's dam?!" Is it "Out with the old" and "In with the new old"?

Not only is it possible that an item that you value highly is no longer an object of desire, but the state of the economy may have put the kibosh on that entire collecting niche. Mama's Beanie Babies (not antiques, obviously, but collectibles), for example, went up in the Beanie Bubble, then went down when the bubble burst, and went even *downer*, if you don't mind the silly word, when the economy tanked. Those who thought they were investing in antiques during the go-go 1990s may have found themselves foundering in white elephants 20 years later. Antiques don't always go up in value, even without a devastating recession.

<u>Market Influences</u>

The antique business – whether you're buying or selling – is inherently one of regrets, as in, "I should have priced it higher; I shouldn't have bought that lime-green Eastlake sofa; I should have waited until the market heated up again for lime-green Eastlake sofas before selling mine..."

Some of the influences on the value of your item are:

◆ The local market: The smallish middle class town I live in, for example, is a terrible place to sell even midrange art, ethnic items, genuine folk art and, frankly, actual antiques. With rare exceptions it's a décor market, and the shabby chic places are doing a booming business in even Made-in-China items, as long as they *look* vintagey.

◆ In your own local market, primitives may be hugely popular, or Royal Doulton tea cups, or kitsch. If what you're selling isn't what the market's buying, though, it may pay off for you to sell your items elsewhere. Your Mid-century Modern table and chairs will do far better in Palm Springs or Palm Beach than, say, Spokane or Little Rock, never mind the problem of getting them there!

◆ The wider market: Even most smaller auction houses are connected to online auction services, so that someone in, say, Minnetonka, Augusta, or Katmandu can bid on the French Impressionist painting you're selling through an auction house in Texas. If the economy as a whole is shuddering and shivering, though, no place will be a great place to sell, no matter how good your merchandise is.

◆ The economy: If you can afford to wait it out to see if gold will go up or Roseville pottery regain its popularity, you may be able to make more money... or possibly less. If your aim, however, is to take the money, clean out the house and run, gambling on the market won't make much sense.

◆ Cultural trends: Whatever they're buying on *American Pickers* (or the next trendy show) is what the market currently wants. For the last few years that's been advertising signs and memorabilia, car stuff, and rusty industrial relics, such as hay pulleys. As noted above, though, those trends don't necessarily translate into sellability if no one in your area wants a hay pulley decorating the living room!

◆ Of special interest to you, the seller, will be the reputation that an auction house or estate liquidator has. Word gets around about iffy practices, and the customers who count may stay away from dicey operations.

◆ Even the weather can have a profound effect. If it happens to snow the night before your estate sale; if there's a sudden sun break in an otherwise gloomy fall... Weather is just another unpredictable factor in the mix.

◆ Timing: There are good times and bad times to sell; for instance in August parents focus on back-to-school, last vacations, etc., and don't think much about antique shopping. Alternately, lore has it that the auction world does well after Christmas. Still, timing is a *maybe* at best and shouldn't be something high on your list to worry about.

Finally, it's all – as they say – a crapshoot! For no reason at all, the hordes show up, stay home, or go dancing at midnight. If it were easy to forecast shopping trends and habits, thousands of MBAs would be out of work!

<u>Why the Marketplace is Changing</u>

"Are you looking for anything in particular?" I ask new customers. "No thanks, I'll just see what speaks to me," is a frequent answer. And the thing that speaks is most often something the customer feels a connection to, something from their past: something they owned, something they wanted, or connected to a memory. It's no surprise that nostalgia is a big player in the antiques market.

The tech generation didn't grow up with pocket watches, post cards, and butter molds (say what?!) as items they'll remember fondly and want to revisit, so, generally, those things have fallen off in popularity. Roy Rogers...? *Roy who?!* Rin Tin Tin? Captain Marvel? There are plenty of kids who've never heard of Mick Jagger, let alone the icons of the past. To watch a black-and-white movie might kill them, and not a soul listens to the foxtrots of yore! So those connections, too, are gone... along with the market for the memorabilia that went with them.

Most younger people have never experienced the romance of steam trains, air travel, or a long sea voyage. There's nothing special about waiting in airport lines nowadays, being shoved on in a herd, and made to pay extra for a bag of peanuts... so why would anyone want to collect airline memorabilia?! I point to the younger folks (under 50 as I write) because while older collectors may still be buying, in general we're thinking more about downsizing and simplifying. It's not as fun to collect stoneware crocks (yes, I have!) once you figure out what it takes to move, store, and display them!

The same holds true for dozens of areas of collecting, from once-popular books (the old Nancy Drew series, for instance) to everyday items of the past, like film cameras, kerosene lamps, and kitchenware.

Looking Back

My mother's generation valued hope chest items. Yes, girls, believe it or not, up until the tradition finally died out in the 1970s, young ladies gathered the nicest dishes, linens, and houseware items they could in hopes of someday being married to a prince and living happily in a wonderland of shiny dishes and happy children. Of course the wonderland part didn't always pan out, but at least even the most unfortunate could be bear the misery while surrounded by the loveliest tablecloths and candlesticks! Whether happy or not, for these marriage misses and Mrs., having one's neighbor admire, envy, and covet one's shiny new toaster was a bonus.

A good wife kept a nice home that often included both a "good" set (probably saved in the hope chest or received as wedding gifts) plus "everyday" items, such as a set of Noritake in the cupboard and Melmac plastic on the table. The best homes boasted best the china, crystal, flatware, and lovely linens they could afford. If a sterling silver tea set was a no-go, a silver-plated one would do. If not plate, well, the five & dime had a perfectly charming china tea pot and the *darlingest* matching cups! While we still convey wealth and status through our things, tastes have radically changed.

The Great Depression and World War II rationing left their marks as households made do with cheaper substitutes for fancy items (if they could afford anything at all beyond the basics). Depression glass in pretty patterns took the place of cut lead crystal. Cotton pillowcases, margarine, pine tables painted with faux wood grain... Utilitarian items such as Bauer and Fiestaware dishes and mixing bowls were made to enjoy and to last in bright colors and plain styles. Infused with the aesthetic of the Arts & Crafts movement – simple, durable, and enjoyable in their own right – these designs turned their back on the statusy statements, and the gaudy frills of Victoriana.

For the first half of the 20ᵗʰ century, women worked hard at scrimping and saving. They canned (and often grew) their own foods, ironed everything, mended everything, and hand-washed all the dishes. A pretty indulgence, such as a vase or picture, bottle of perfume or crystal pickle dish was prized and taken care of and often passed down as an heirloom. Items weren't made to use and toss.

It's no surprise, then, that the daughters of these women also cared for these things. There was a great nostalgia for the kerosene lamps that Granddad read by, and for Mom's darning eggs, embroidered linens, and hand-tatted hankies. Sons collected their dads'-era military memorabilia, and coveted sports and work items of all kinds.

The men's stuff has probably suffered the least, marketwise, as we still have wars, guys (and gals, too, of course) still fish and play football, and still prize old tools for both utility and nostalgia.

When I opened my store I expected to see The Train Guys – men like my dad and his friends, who had family connections to the railroad and loved everything about trains and train travel, from switch keys to dining-car china. But those collectors have dwindled. Excepting toy trains, there's little demand in my store for the memorabilia that filled my dad's man cave. Menus, postcards, ashtrays and photos are still awaiting buyers. There are still collectors out there, but the market has shrunk.

There are exceptions to all of the above, no doubt: rabid collectors of hand mixers, darning eggs, monocles, and butter churns surely exist. They're not the mainstream buyers anymore, though.

Adventures in the Junk Trade: The Ins & the Outs

A lady in her 60s, a walking crazy quilt of a gal, comes huffing and puffing into the store, an orange paisley scarf trailing sadly in the heat. She's toting a huge flowered bag. Her red hair shimmers like the waves of a mirage as her blue eyes scan the shop. She has stuff to sell, she says, it's in her trunk, and she promises it's not a 60-piece set of china. No, she tells me with a flip of her hair, she's devoted her entire adult life to collecting... wooden potato mashers. (If you haven't seen one: they look like miniature caveman clubs, maybe a foot long, total. Just wood. Very plain.) Curiosity wins out over logic, and I follow her out to a big old Buick where she pops the trunk to reveal a huge box jam-packed with 'em like driftwood piled up on a desolate beach. My my, I think. They all look about the same: chunky, wooden. Lacking personality. I wonder what sort of kinky mashed-potato fetish has driven this particular obsession. Maybe it's the butter.

"Well," I sigh as I attempt in vain to appreciate them. "Hmmm..."

She picks out one and then another, holding each one up in the sunlight to point out its special features: "Look at this one," she says, glancing over to see if I'm admiring it properly. "Late 1800s... beautiful shape... And it has such interesting paint remnants. Doesn't it?!" she demands, clutching it by its wooden throat. "Oh, yes, yes, of course. Very interesting!*" I surreptitiously check the street to see if there'll be witnesses should she throw me in there and slam the lid.*

"And this one has a slightly different curve and an extra-nice patina. Seeee?!" She's a walking exclamation point. If she had a shiv, she'd be fingering it in her apron pocket. "Incredible, right?!" Oh, heck, yeah, it's incredible! "I'm only asking five bucks apiece for the whole lot," she coos roughly into my ear, suddenly boasting the mysterioso Spanish-accented voice of Edward James Olmos. "Eh, homes?" I expect her to say next, suddenly a streetwise antiques freak.

"Jeepers... no, thanks," I mutter gingerly. It's always hard to break a crazy lady's heart. "But two or three," I offer. "They're primitives and that's hot right now. Sure, I'll buy two or three. That'd be great." ... a small price to pay to lessen her trunkload of ammunition should her late-night thoughts turn to tossing them through my plate-glass window...as any self-respecting potato-masher-collector would do should she suspect that a smarmy antique dealer was dissing her phat collection of down-home spuds crushers.

"Oh, no no no!" Her irises spin like daggers toward a target, her hair sticking out as if electrified by the horror of the idea. High dudgeon radiates off her like skunk stink. "I couldn't break up the collection!"

What? It takes me a minute to get what she's saying. "Oh. Right," I answer. "You'll probably want to find someone who'll appreciate it all." What I don't tell her is that there is no such person anywhere on earth except her in a parallel universe. Or maybe someone in a little town on the prairie where they bludgeon pesky varmints with collectible clubs.

The moral to the story? Sometimes it makes sense to take what you can get. I picture her driving around, to this day, from town to town, store to store, her paisley scarf flapping out the window as she hunts in vain for that one person who loves potato mashers as much as she does.

What's Hot / What's Not

In addition to wooden potato mashers, if you're deaccessioning any of the following, you may be surprised by the fall in the market: comic books; lacework; dolls; china; silver plate; Coke and other soda pop memorabilia; glass and dishes of all kinds; linens; stamps; post cards; matchbooks and advertising ashtrays; '40s-'50s kitchen stuff, including salt and pepper sets, trivets, and gadgets; Hummels and other figurines; stoneware (here in the West, that is); pottery such as McCoy, Shawnee, and Roseville; Westmoreland, Heisey, carnival and other glassware. Every locale is a little different, though, as is every antique store. My friends up the street still sell high-end glass to their longtime customers, while I can't give it away free with a box of Duz!

As previously mentioned, advertising, gas-station and auto-related items are also hot, as are vintage Halloween and Christmas decorations, photos that feature interesting subject matter, pre-1970s TV Guides, and better costume jewelry. Antique medical and scientific items, such as hydrometers and compasses, are also in demand. (And yes, a customer has requested "brains in a jar." If you have any of those...!) And, as always, Civil War items can fetch a good price. Political memorabilia from that era, though, not so much. "Tippecanoe and Tyler Too"? More recent political posters, buttons, and bumper stickers do well in my store.

It's hard to say what younger folks are buying, though tiki mugs and carvings have been popular now for 20 years. Glass floats appeal to all, as well as Indian artifacts and arts, 1950s bar ware, movie memorabilia, Western collectibles such as spurs and artwork, Art Deco and Bakelite items. (This is what my recent experience tells me, though it could easily be off the mark for your area. My store is only 15 minutes away from Portland, Oregon, across the river, but what I can sell and the prices I can ask are wildly different!)

I've consistently done well with taxidermy, sterling rings, pottery wall pockets, vintage glasses frames, decorative boxes, and a variety of pictures and mirrors. The rest, though, has been unpredictable.

Chapter 7:   Getting a Clue

Adventures in the Junk Trade: Get Smart!

This afternoon, a couple in their 40s – he scruffy, round, and tough; she fake-eyelashed, rounder and tougher – set a great old leather carrying case on my counter. The worn exterior sported travel decals from the 1800s, and the interior held a fine black top hat, beautifully preserved. They wanted to sell it, but didn't say why. I did the Ebay routine, searching out and showing them a nearly identical hat and case that sold for $75. I offered them $100. It was more than I should pay, I told them, but I loved the items and believed that I could sell them at an upcoming antiques show for a little more than that. I was feeling very generous at that point... only to be told by the wife, in her brassy blonde voice, that in no way could they take less than two hundred dollars, as she'd paid $250 for the hat and box just a few months ago! Hmmm. "You wildly overpaid," I wanted to say, finishing handily with, "you silly cow." But I didn't.

The husband asked about a Winchester sign I had, and I offered to trade straight across, though the sign was priced slightly higher. Again: I was being rather saintlike and deserved a bow or at least a tip of the top hat. Ha! He said yes, and we were ready to swap. "Well, I want something, too!" she bawled, a big old 42-year-old baby!

"Sorry," I said. "That's the best I can do."

After loads of accusatory whining, and me unwilling to budge, she bought a child's wooden block for $3 and they waltzed out of the store in a huff. Goodbye, great old hat.

The moral to the story: You can want what you want all you want, but you won't get what you want unless what you want is what the dealer is willing to pay. Do you want the (hat, sugar shakers, drill bits, gewgaws, or gimcracks) or do you want the money? You can cling to the idea of "what it's worth" or you can take a hit if necessary and walk away with what you can get.

Today I'm listing Roseville pottery pieces on Ebay for less than I paid for them. I can't sell them at a profit, they're taking up space, and it's time for them to go. It does me no good to cling to them, trying in vain to recoup what I can't. *Let it go!*

The more you know about what you have, as well as how much it's worth, the more powerful you'll be as you sell it. More than once I've sold what I thought was a Gewgaw only to find out it was not only a Whatnot, but a valuable Whatnot at that! :-(Alas!

If you're selling things as fast as possible or if you have too many things to deal with, you might not care what you have, exactly, or how much you get. If that's the case, just skip ahead.

Be Your Own Appraiser

Professional appraisals are the usual means of finding out values of things, from a single marble to an entire estate's worth of items. They can be expensive, so before we get there, let's see if it will pay for you to do your own evaluating.

Step 1: Ebay

Ebay is my go-to resource when pricing my own goods, assessing the worth of what's being sold to me, or deciding whether an item at an auction or store is priced low enough for me to buy it. In general, antique stores charge more for the same item than Ebay does (for instance, a tea pot on Ebay might cost $14 plus shipping. In the antique store it may be priced at $28), but in my middlebrow neck of the antiques world I try to stay competitive, particularly as more people bring smart phones into the store, or take photos of an item so that they can look up prices at home. Thus, checking the Completed Listings box on Ebay is a good start in deciding how much your item is worth.

You must be registered on Ebay in order to do this, which merely takes a credit card in order to set up an account. If you're trying to price (or identify) a pair of glass candlesticks, you'll search for "glass candlesticks," check the Completed Listings box on the left, then narrow your search as much as possible. "Glass Candlesticks" might be narrowed down to "Green Antique Dolphin Cambridge Candlesticks," for instance, once you've found the candlesticks that match yours. Selling results can often be all over the place, with the same pair going for $12 one day, $3 the next, and $50 the next week. Tossing out the extreme results should help you to find a reasonable value. (There are lots of resources on how to use Ebay, should you need to learn the basics.)

There are other online sales and auction sites, of course, but Ebay is the Big Kahuna, and almost always yields results. Books and better art come to mind as selling areas that do better elsewhere.

Step 2: Most areas of collecting have online experts (often bloggers), specialty sellers, or collectors clubs. Should you find yourself trying to identify and price a round brass *thingie*, for instance, an Ebay search might tell you that it's an English horse brass (bridle decoration), what a horse brass is, a price range, and possibly its age. A further Google search might help you find antique stores that specialize in British items, or it might lead you to an Anglophile group that can assist with more details or wider knowledge. While the younger generation is surely rolling its eyes and muttering, "Duh" right about now, for those of us who didn't grow up with computers, it's not always an obvious place to look.

Step 3: Dozens of auctions take place both live and online every day. (See "Chapter 15: The Weird Auction World.") The benefit to the general public is that there are auction results for just about anything sold, from a handful of hat pins to a trompe l'oeil cabinet. Specialty auctions focus on European paintings, farm machinery, all the contents of a pizzeria, you name it, and you can access the final sale price of these items at no cost, with a little persistence, which will give you a clue about what *your* items are worth. Just now, having recently sold a large Limoges vase, I Googled "Auction results Limoges" and within seconds was viewing Skinner auction house's 881 sales results for a variety of Limoges china pieces. I've found several vases similar to mine, and it looks as though I might have made more money on my vase by sending it to an auction house. I wanted to sell it quickly, though, which I did on Ebay; I made a profit, and it was easily done.

You can also find web sites that offer auction results for a fee. A place called Invaluable, for instance, offers prices realized from a variety of auctions, saving you the trouble of checking all over the internet. The company charges $20 a month or $200 a year for results dating back only 12 months... and you have to register your email address with them just to find out that they're going to charge you! Pricier subscriptions offer more extensive and older archives. As you're trying to make money, not spend it, the value of one of these services would be questionable.

Individual auction houses don't charge to show the results of their auctions. The catch is that you'll have to spend volumes of time checking archives to find the results of a particular item.

Finally, sites such as Auctionzip.com, Proxibid.com, and LiveAuctioneers.com "broadcast" auctions live over the internet, and give you good information about who's auctioning what, when. If you want to price that Limoges vase, you might search for an auction that offers high-quality china, then check the archive of that auction house.

The results of one sale may not help you much, however – if the sale occurred in Akron in 2007 in the winter, and you're selling your vase in Tampa in 2015 in the summer, you may end up with a skewed idea of what you can get, so the more results you can find, the better.

Here's a real-life example of how it can work:

A year ago, a picker brought in a trio of brass candlesticks. (Illustration 1) The narly old patina on them makes them seem old, but even if they didn't belong to Henry VIII, I still like their interesting look and they're pieces I've never seen before. I paid $8 each for them, a good price, I thought, never mind that I haven't sold a candlestick since I opened. Surely *some*one would recognize their value! I have them priced (as I write this) at $16 apiece, and they've now been taking up valuable table space ever since.

Meanwhile, as I was tooling around Ebay today, I ran across candlesticks that look nearly identical. The seller described them as: "Rare Pair of 17th Century Brass Pricket Church Candlesticks or Candle Spikes. The Candlesticks show great early form and I am sure they would be English or Dutch in origin. I have done my best to show the Candlesticks apart to show the turning, the bolt portions are all Hand Turned on a Lathe, which is consistent with them being very early examples."

(Never mind that the auction title was for "French" candlesticks, the bad grammar alone might've tipped me off to her lack of knowledge!) The bid on her auction was already nearly $400 – so did I have a treasure or were mine lesser reproductions or simply newer? I sent a message to the dealer, asking how she determined the age and origin (beyond "I was told they were found in a Church in Quebec about 40 years ago," as her auction listing said. Told by whom? Reminder to self: Online, no one can hear you scream!) She responded by sending me a link to an antique store's offering that looked somewhat similar to hers, but not a whole lot. She also sent me a note: " I was told they are either French or Dutch. There has been 400 views and no one has emailed to tell me I am wrong LOL." Four hundred people had looked, dozens had bid, and she was

LOL-ing all the way to the bank! She was relying on strangers to tell her if she was right or not. Honestly, I had to find out if I was missing out on the big bucks.

With 15 minutes more of online sleuthing, I found, at a British antique shop, nearly identical candlesticks listed as being Italian (illustration 2) … and Wikipedia information on the history of screws. "English instrument maker Jesse Ramsden (1735–1800) was working on the toolmaking and instrument-making end of the screw-cutting problem, and in 1777 he invented the first satisfactory screw-cutting lathe." I never thought I'd need to know this! Well, her candlesticks still could have been made earlier, with an *un*satisfactory screw-cutting lathe, but at this point I decided she was very good at sounding like she knew what she was talking about… without really knowing a thing.

 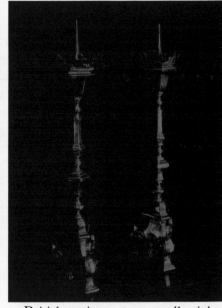

My candlesticks, worth about $8   British antique store candlesticks, worth a fortune!

After mulling over the whole shebang, I've decided that my own brass candlesticks are *extremely* old, IMPORTANT (as the high-end auction

world likes to describe various bits of flotsam), remarkable, *superior*...
and worth about 8 bucks apiece!

A couple morals to the story may make a difference in your approach to
getting advice on the value of your items:

◆ Just because someone sounds authoritative doesn't mean squat!

◆ It might be worth your time to double-check what someone tells
you

◆ Keep your nose open for the smell of pants on fire.

Finally: It's probably easier than you think to find out what you have
and place an approximate value on it. Even if you only come up with a
wild ballpark idea, it's better than being in the "not-a-clue" club.

Professional Appraisals

Dozens of online appraisal sites will pop up with a simple "antique
appraisal" Google search. They range from free to about $45 per item,
with a variety of approaches. One site has an archive of thousands of
items. You type in, say, "Dog collar," and photos of matching items will
pop up. Once you find an exact match of the dog collar you'd like
appraised, you pay to find out how much the item in the photo is worth.
(It's not specified when or where these valuations originally happened;
they could be wildly out of date, and very-off-the-mark for the current
times and circumstances.) The odd catch is that you supply your credit
card first, and then you're charged a fee, from about $2 up to $10,
depending on the value of the pictured item. But you won't know how
much you'll be charged ahead of time! It's a peculiar system... and I
found no results whatsoever for "dog collar." (Hard to believe, but yep,
there are dog collar collectors!)

Other sites offer appraisals based on emailed photos and descriptions. I
can't speak from experience about the accuracy of online appraisals, but
my first admittedly snobby opinion is that they could be a very

expensive waste of time and money, particularly as you're likely dealing with a good number of items.

In-person appraisals can be necessary for probate, estate valuations, proving the value of charitable contributions, family disputes, insurance matters, etc., but appraisers charge like lawyers do: A typical fee for an on-site estate appraisal is $250 for the first hour and $150 for every hour after that. In addition, you might pay $75 an hour for travel and another $75 an hour for research.

Should you have one or two higher-end pieces that you and your siblings are playing tug-of-war over, a per-item appraisal might be helpful. These can range from a verbal evaluation, with the prices varying accordingly, up to $45 or for an item, more if much research needs to be done. Written appraisals will include photos and a detailed description of the item, and will note whether the appraisal is for fair-market (auction), retail, or replacement (insurance) value.

How to Choose an Appraiser

The American Society of Appraisers, the Appraisers Association of America, and the International Society of Appraisers are the largest certifying organizations, totaling thousands of members worldwide. Most certifications demand a college degree, specialized classes, years of experience, and examinations. Members of each are accredited in different areas of expertise, such as gems & jewelry, personal property, and real property. Beyond that, each expert will have his or her own area of interest and particular knowledge, such as Early American glass, or pre-20th-century textiles. Ask what an appraiser's specialty is. While they're all trained in research methods, as long as you're paying the big bucks, you ought to get the most out of it!

The Appraisers Association of America notes that its members' job is to: "provide independent valuation outside of third party influences; retain no outside interest in the subject property other than an accurate and professional value; contract for appraisal work only within the areas of their professional expertise; reach objective value conclusions by considering all factors in appraisal standards; use the highest standards of connoisseurship in examining and documenting property; professional remuneration is independent of the value of the subject property."

In other words, an appraiser's fee shouldn't have any connection to the value of the object being looked at. Likewise, it's entirely unethical for an appraiser to make an offer on an item that he or she has just appraised. My own customers occasionally request an appraisal – but most antique dealers aren't qualified (including myself). At most I'll offer an opinion, and that's probably the most you should expect without paying for an official look.

Adventures in the Junk Trade: Taking My Own Advice

It's easy to tell other people how to do things, particularly how to run their lives. You know, the small things! Following my own advice is another ball of wax, though. I keep telling my sister, "If you want peace of mind, just clean the house from top to bottom once a week." Of course I never do that. It's silly advice, impossible to do, really, if you lead a normal life, and it just wouldn't make anyone's mind peaceful. (Wouldn't you just worry about new dust? So keep it dusty, I say!)

Meanwhile, I've filled pages here with directions on how you can get rid of those pesky valuable antiques... but can I follow that advice myself? I'm going to see what happens when I do:

A couple of days ago here at the store, a lovely, well-dressed woman in her early 40s stood in front of my counter and lied to me baldfaced about a bag of Asian seals she had (also called chops or stamps, they're often small pillars of carved stone with an animal on the top and the artist's mark on the bottom, which is inked and used to sign artwork. There are also stamps for train stations, museums, government offices, etc. – just like old-fashioned rubber stamps, only hand made, sometimes out of wood, brass or other material).

In a wan voice, she calmly said it was her son's collection. She smiled like a tipsy woman on a heaving ship clinging bravely to a railing. Her son was in the car, waiting, she said, then touched her orange poof of hair, which matched her orange camelhair coat. Of course at that point I had a dozen piercing questions, but my greed won out and I didn't ask them. Instead, I dipped into her gleaming red gift bag – the kind you put Christmas presents in – with the same sort of "What did Santy Claus bring?" anticipation. Wow! There were about a dozen seals of varying sizes, each one different, and each one wrapped in the same kind of plastic bag that our local newspapers are delivered in. (Aha! First clue: collector reads the paper, must be smart!) There was a small brass cow, a tall pottery mountain, a clear red dragon (plastic? Resin?), carved stone pieces, very old-looking flat bronze stamps, several made from wood, and finally, a pottery frog that rattled. The frog doesn't look Asian, and the bottom appears to have Mayan writing on it... so I've decided that it's pre-Columbian and probably priceless. The Asian items, though, surely have a value, and I want to know what it is.

As I looked, I casually asked, "Has your son been to Asia?"

"Oh, no, I don't ... uh... think so," she answered.

"Do you mind if I ask why he's selling these things?"

She gave me a little wink. "Gambling problem," she said in that same bland voice, not the least bit embarrassed for her apparently miserable and mucked-up little offspring.

"I see," I said, mostly seeing nothing but a lotta hooey. "How much do you want for them?"

"Oh, I don't know. I'll have to ask him." She didn't move to ask him. I considered whether I should look them up on Ebay and make her an offer based on what I found, as I often do. She didn't look like she cared what I did, as long as I forked over some money pretty soon. She gave me the creeps with her teetering Stepford Wives demeanor, and I wanted her to leave. "$400 or so," she said.

"That's way out of my ballpark!" I blurted. I love shouting at customers about how broke I am! I have a pretty small ballpark, in fact, but I'd had a good week and had some extra batters in the dugout. "How about $200?" She jumped at it. Done and done until she said, "How about $225?" Just as we settled on $210, the "son" popped his head in the door. He was about 38 to her 42, unshaven and stupid looking. He was clearly not a newspaper reader!

The next day, the very small angel on my left shoulder – the one with the booming voice – shouted WHAT THE HAY and so I called the cops and reported that I had what I believed to be stolen property. I also put an ad on Craigslist, and though I've received some sad queries in the last couple of weeks, no one has claimed the seals as theirs. Now I need to sell them, never mind that I'm certain that they were a carefully collected lot and are probably being mourned even as I write this. I'm picturing an academic loner with Coke-bottles glasses… this collection being his lifetime's work, he's beating himself with his fists, cursing the gods, and weeping uncontrollably. Sigh! It's better, I decide, that I'm the keeper of the treasure rather than the scurvy meth addict and his pale mol.

Step One: Appraising the seals myself

First: Check Ebay for comparable items. After looking at pages of seals, I don't know any more than when I started. There are various stamps priced both high and low, from $4 for a "jade" animal stamp with free shipping from Shanghai (it looks like one of the cheap carved onyx donkeys you find in Tijuana), to hundreds of dollars for one that looks not that different to me. Clearly, I don't know what I'm looking at and I don't know how to judge these pieces. I do know that the Chinese are expert at 1) making beautiful artworks of all kinds, and 2) faking beautiful artworks of all kinds. Is the "Jade Buddha Bust Love Seal" the real thing? The price is $73.91. Ninety-one cents? It's coming from Guangzhou, Canton, China. Maybe the change is for a sandwich for the mailman.

How about the "Vintage Hand Carved Chinese Squirrel Soapstone Wax Seal"? He's got the longest squirrel arms I've ever seen! Also, next to the Chinese writing on the bottom is the name "Roddy." Next!

By the time I get to "Chinese Antique Nephrite Jade Powerful Huge Beast Love Seal Statue Carving" I'm getting the blues. This one's priced at $135.20, and it looks as poorly carved as the Mexican donkey.

The most interesting seal I find is a crazy-looking little animal, marketed as "Very nice Very Rare! Yuan Dyn. Bronze lion seal- Jin Feng." The opening bid is $1,200 and the seller swears, "We don't sell any fake Antiques! High-quality service and good prestige are our commitment to you! 100% Genuine guarantee!!! Please rest assured to buy!"

That would certainly seal the deal if I were a buyer (!) but I've decided that Ebay isn't telling me anything useful about the collection I have.

Before leaving the page, I decide to bid on the "RARE COLLECTIBLES WITH CARVED DRAGON CHINESE OLD ANTIQUE JADE SEAL." After all, it's only $8 with free shipping. Treasure? If not, well, sheesh, don't I have a baby shower to buy a gift for? What baby wouldn't want this?! (When it arrives, weeks later, it looks like it was manufactured in a Chicago slaughterhouse, a chunk of brown bone dug into to look very vaguely like a roadkill dragon.)

Step Two: Online research

After Googling "antique seal" I've ended up at LiveAuctioneers.com, a site that broadcasts (online) auctions live from venues all over the country. Once on the site, an easy search for "seal" brings up dozens of offerings from various upcoming auctions. The photos are clear and the page well laid out. Best of all, there's an obvious button marked "Sold." Bingo! I can check completed auctions for final prices, and if I'm lucky I'll find seals very similar to mine. To see those auction results it's necessary to create an account... alas!... but this one is painless, quick, and doesn't ask for a credit card number.

In less than five minutes I'm checking out the auction results for antique seals, and I'm heartened by what I find. The "sold" prices are better than those on Ebay, perhaps because the items were offered by auction houses that are presumed to be reputable, rather than by an utterly unknowable Chinese entity. On each page are the final prices of 20 different items... which may be items sold at 20 different auction houses. It quickly becomes obvious that this would be a good way to find an auction house appropriate for selling my seals.

If the seals weren't so different from one another and so hard to assess in photos – let alone considering my advanced degree in Huh? – I might be able to take a guess at what I have and what it's worth. But, as the Snookis of the world might agree: fugeddaboudit! I'm still not getting that necessary clue.

Another dealer has stopped by my shop, one who's constantly telling me fish stories about his big sales of high-end art. If anyone might have a referral to an Asian-arts appraiser, it should be him. I spend 10 minutes explaining the challenge, anticipating a gem from his snobbish mouth. "Look on Ebay," he says sagely. "You don't have to know what it's worth." Yes, I know. But I want to know something about what I have. I want to know that that smartypants appraiser on Antiques Roadshow *would value the collection at "eight to ten thousand. Conservatively." Is that so much to ask?*

Step Three: Plan B

The self-appraisal has given me a ballpark figure of about $49 for a stamp... anywhere from 99 cents to $440, with $49 being a popular figure seen on the Ebay pics. Looking around on Google and elsewhere has given me some information about the history of the stamps and their uses, but I still feel at a loss. I decide to take a chance and send photos of the group to Auction House A on the East Coast. I sold a painting through them a couple of years ago, so of course we're BFFs and they'll help me out. Right?

Three or Four Months Later: Haven't heard a word! There's clearly a bad habit in the auction world of ignoring the idea of customer service. I recently attempted to hire a well-known appraiser (aka Shell Out a Lotta My Hard-Earned Bucks!) to look at some masks that I'm curious about. Via email, he asked a couple of questions, then just... forgot about me. After answering his questions I never heard from him again, regardless that I wanted to pay him for his expertise. All I can say is wottev. If it happens to you, don't take it personally as rudeness is clearly the norm. Life is short; move on, I tell myself.

Just as I gave up on hearing anything from Auction House A, I noticed an ad in the local paper: Auction House B was hosting an appraisal day for Chinese artworks, meaning they were looking for items to auction. It couldn't hurt to send them photos of my seals, so I did, imagining a lot of laughter on the other end! To my surprise they contacted me a couple of days later, offered to come to my store to see the seals so that I wouldn't have to take time off, and then arrived, on time, with a coordinator and two appraisers in tow. They were extremely nice, spent time looking around, and actually bought a few things... after one of them asked for a discount on a $7 road map! It was $2 worth of entertainment to have a high-end appraiser request a discount on such a small item. He deals with priceless artwork and incredibly valuable antiques every day, and he surely gets paid more in a year than my shop will make in my lifetime... (Do you think they'll discount the seller's commission I'll be paying them if the seals sell? Very funny!) The group of them were exceptionally pleasant and left without once pointing out that my prints of big-eyed children aren't exactly antiques! Most importantly, they took the seals on consignment to be auctioned, they said, in October, about three months away. (As I currently write this, it's February 2014 and I've been told – after pestering them – that the seals will be auctioned at the end of the month. Should you go this route, be prepared to wait!)

If your estate holdings had included the seals, it would clearly have been more efficient to have them sold through an estate service, to an antiques dealer, or even on Ebay, though those methods would have *earned you less money than the auction estimate of about $1,200 that I've been given. The moral to this story, as I see it is: There's no right or wrong way to deaccession any items that you need to have gone, just faster or slower, with more regret or less.*

CHAPTER 8: YOU CAN'T MAKE MONEY WITHOUT SPENDING SOME

Geez, how I love to hate those *Picker/Roadshow/Storage Wars* shows on TV! "What a crock," I curse as the little old lady clutches her pounding heart at the news that her Louis the 14th bidet is worth $40,000. "Now what?!" I swear at the TV. "How the heck is she going to sell it for that much?! *Poor old thing,* she's gonna die heartbroken, clinging to her cold bidet, and it's your fault, Keno Brothers!" The answer is: she can't make what they've told her it's worth unless she knows someone personally who'll pony up, or is approached on the street because she's now the famous Bidet Gal who fainted in Leigh Keno's arms.

If you've seen *American Pickers*, you've seen the toted-up figures at the end: "Paid $100, will re-sell for $400." Ka-ching! Done and done! Nice going, fellas! But what they don't show you is Mike & Frank spending gas money to find their treasure and haul it home, then spending time cleaning it up and repairing it, paying overhead to display it and have Danielle mind the store, dusting the thing, swearing at it when blind drunk and in a rage that they can't pay the rent, and then having it sit on the shelf for possibly months until they pay more money to haul it away somewhere, maybe back to the hoarder's garage that it came from. On the occasion that they have something appraised, they never count that as an expense, such as "Paid appraiser $250 for an hour to learn our circus poster's worth... $225!" (It is, however, swell entertainment!)

There's an auction show that I enjoy, but unfortunately, when they add up the proceeds at the end – "Mark was hoping for $400 for his bobcat rug, and we sold it for $425! Mark's going home a happy man!"— they don't include the sellers commission, probably 30% on that bobcat rug. Poor Mark got more like $300!

So it's important to keep in mind that it costs money to sell your items. Excepting Craigslist or a garage sale, you'll be giving up from 10% to 50% or more of the retail value of any one item. It may sound bad, but the services you're paying for will most likely make that cost worth it: ease in selling, safety, a bigger market, etc.

Adventures in the Junk Trade: What Goes Around...

A skinny Native American man I'll call Eddie occasionally brings things into my store to sell me. He's as gnarled as a beach-washed tree branch. He could be 45 or 75; it's hard to tell by looking at the features that reflect a rumble of a life that likely includes jail, booze, and plenty of hard times. His eyes are soft, and his voice mellow, though: he's not a bad guy, and he's quite likable.

When I first meet Eddie he's trying to raise money for a place for himself and his teenage son to live, he says, so they don't have to sleep in the car. On another day his son has disappeared and Eddie's afraid for him: the boy lives "in both sexes," he says, dressing as a female. Several days later I spot a tall kid who looks just like Eddie, wearing a sarong, and a headband with a feather stuck straight up, flapper-style.

Eddie's sold me a ring set with turquoise and a bear claw, and a bird-spotting scope, the better to watch eagles, he says, describing his own long days down on the river. It sounds like something a Disneyland Indian would say, I think to myself, but the scope is nice and so is Eddie, so I buy it. But do I believe him? Having dealt with a number of friends and relatives who've become addicts and liars living by their wits and thievery... no, not necessarily. He's likable but I've heard so many tall tales by now that I don't wholly trust anyone who sells things to me.

Let's skip ahead to Mr. X, an average customer, middle aged, middle class, tall and well turned out in a North Face jacket for the Washington drizzle. As I hear the bells on the door tinkle, I'm halfway back in the store talking to someone when I glance up to see him coming in. Before I can call out Hello, he's already talking to me as if I'm standing right there: something about having lost his magic, his daughter can help him get it back, everything was lost in a flood, and he's on his way to a homeless shelter. I'm about to phone 9-1-1 when he tells me he has some dementia but that he knows where he's going today and how he's going to get there. All will be fine, he says, if he can only find the things he needs to set him on his way.

In no time he's pointed to a ring that features an enamel triangle, and to a brass compass, and then a pair of glass dice. He relaxes as he pays for them: now he can get his magic back, he says. I wonder if he's pulling my leg with the hokey purchases, but his singlemindedness is impressive. I consider whether I should call a social service agency or... no, he's confident about things now, and the bills in his wallet show me he can afford a motel room if he needs it. He tucks the items away in various pockets of his parka and he's gone.

A couple of days later Eddie's back. He has something special to show me, he says. His voice is the river of the ages, his worn hands evocative of time immemorial, of hands that picked berries along the banks, and speared salmon in the Columbia. His obsidian eyes look deep into mine as he tugs a suede pouch from inside his coat. "It was my friend's father's father's back 300 years," he says reverently, and I'm back there with him, 300 years away, the sunlight dappling the current through a breeze. The small package, wrapped in suede and tied with a leather thong, balances in his hand. For good measure, he adds: "And his father's before that." Hmm... I can't wait... He unties the laces and flips the package open. To reveal...

"Eddie," I say with a huge sigh, "I just sold that compass two days ago!"

He blinks unbelievingly, his stony eyes sinking to the bottom of the river. "No!"

"Yeah," I say, examining the compass. "Exact same."

"No.....!" A beat. "That guy owed me a lotta money!" As the dawn rose in Eddie's eyes, I got a glimpse of the deal-gone-wrong, probably at the homeless shelter, the "demented" Mr. X trading his ancient compass...

Poor Eddie, his face fallen and his pockets empty! He just can't get over it, he says, that Mr. X took him like that! I buy the compass from Eddie for $8, half of what I sold it for.

The compass is a phony antique from tip to toe, I point out, its brass case smeared with a strange crusted facsimile patina, its dial unnaturally aged and pitted. I'd like not to be taken again.

"I told him that," I tell Eddie. "It's still cool, but think about it," I explain: if the compass were old the brass would be worn down, not diminished under a shmear of varnish, and the dial is under glass, so there's no reason for it to age like that. "That's why I sold it to the guy for 16 dollars instead of 45."

"Yeah," he nods, but that's not what matters to him now. "I gotta find that guy!"

I'm guessing the not-so-demented Mr. X has moved on to greener pastures, his magic now in full flower.

And the moral of the story is: Objects in mirror may be closer than they appear!

PART II: LET THE SELLING GAMES BEGIN!

Now to the nitty gritty: the variety of ways you can sell (or give away) those estate items. It may turn out that you'll decide to keep half, sell most, give 78%, keep another 2/3, and allow your greedy cousin to poke around after it's all been gone through. Whether you'll want to auction a few high-quality items, hold a garage sale for the junk, and sell the Model T on Craigslist will be easier to decide once you read up on the details – the pros and cons; the costs in time and money; and things to watch out for – of each method of deaccessioning.

All manner of items can be liquidated via any of the following methods, from average household furniture, to vintage magazines, to high-end art. The lone specialty area I'm covering here is jewelry, as selling gold, silver and gems carries challenges that no other category does.

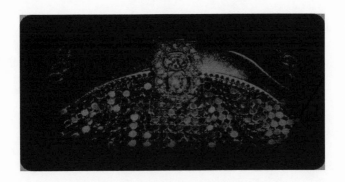

CHAPTER 9: HOW TO SELL JEWELRY, GOLD AND SILVER

There are two ways to look at any fine jewelry you want to sell: as simply metal + stones, or as an entire piece. A sterling bracelet, for example, may be worth only $10 in silver, but sell at upwards of $100 if it's artist-designed, vintage, or especially desirable for whatever reason.

With the recent boom in gold and silver prices, there's also been a boom in reselling perfectly good jewelry (and other items made of silver or gold) that was scrapped by its owner for the metal value alone. A great deal of the jewelry found on Ebay, for instance, is rings, chains, etc., salvaged from the melt heap, and I've personally purchased great jewelry for my store from silver dealers who paid by the ounce for it from a smelter.

The take-away is that good jewelry should garner you more than its scrap value. That said, every pawn shop, antique store, and jewelry store will have a different idea of what they want to pay for fine jewelry, particularly if it's set with diamonds or other stones. (Same with other items made of silver or gold, including watches.) Asking for estimates at several stores (not appraisals) is the way to go in order to get an idea of what your piece can fetch. Shop around before accepting an offer.

An appraisal can be expensive (from $45-$100), but it may be worth it to discover that Aunt Jenny's costume bracelet – the one you thought was chrome and rhinestones – is actually platinum and diamonds! Be sure to specify what value you'd like the appraisal for. Insurance value is quite a bit more than fair-market value. (See "Chapter 7: Getting a Clue.")

While most jewelry stores appraise gold and gems, make sure that any diamond is looked at by an appraiser certified by either the American Gem Society or the American Society of Appraisers. They can also identify stones for you.

How Can You Tell If It's Real Gold or Sterling?

In general, all sterling and gold will be marked: *.925* or *sterling* (or hallmarked, depending on where it was made); 10k, 14k, etc., for gold. An exception is artist-made jewelry, particularly Native American sterling rings and bracelets, which may be marked with an initial, a symbol, or often not at all. *.800* denotes a lesser-quality silver.

EPS, Quadruple Plated, and other mystery marks on silver are used to indicate electroplating, or silver plate. There's no silver-scrap value in plated pieces. Likewise, *gold filled* means a gold layer bonded to a base metal such as brass. *Gold Layered, HGE* and similar markings indicate that the piece isn't solid gold and has no scrap value.

Beware: I've owned brass bracelets marked "14k," and ".925" bracelets that weren't silver at all. Silver from Mexico and China should be tested. "Alpaca" silver isn't, and neither is "German silver," which is an alloy of copper, nickel, and zinc.

How Much You Should Get

A reputable antique-jewelry store might give you as much as 70% of the value they believe they can sell the item for. You might be offered, for instance, $50-$75 for a ring they believe they can sell for $100. On the other hand, a pawn shop or less reputable store might offer you relatively little or tell you that it's only worth scrap.

A website called Silverrecyclers.com offers up-to-the minute prices being offered for scrap gold and silver. On their scrap calculator you input the weight and type of metal you have, and it'll instantly show you what the value is. There's no cost and it's easy to use, but you do need a scale that can weigh in grams. (Inexpensive to purchase on Amazon.com.) Should the scrap price for sterling be 50 cents a gram today, a jeweler or gold buyer should pay you 40% to 50% (for the metal only; stones will be removed), or about 50 cents for a two-gram ring. That's because the person who takes it in will only be paid by the smelter about 80% of the full scrap price.

If you have a great deal of scrap, you can skip the middleman and go directly to the smelter. The smelter I visit requires a minimum of $200 in scrap value for the general public to be allowed to sell there. They'll buy not only scrap jewelry, but gold dental work... so don't toss Uncle Joe's fancy bridge and crowns!

Costume Jewelry

There can be more unnoticed value in a junk box of old costume jewelry than you suspect! A Miriam Haskell necklace I purchased at a garage sale last year for a dollar sold online for more than a hundred. If you're not familiar with the varieties of costume jewelry and their values, have someone knowledgeable look through yours. An antique store or lower- to mid-range auction would be a good choice for selling if you have nicer pieces. (And, as always, you can post items on Ebay for little to nothing and let the market set the price. Sometimes offering a number of pieces as a single lot will better your chances for bids, especially if there isn't a single standout piece.) "Signed" pieces (simply meaning that there's a maker's name) can bring hundreds of dollars apiece, depending on the company, the design, etc.

What to look for: better jewelry will be well constructed and solid. Stones will be set in prongs rather than glued in. They'll be shiny and fresh looking. (Older paste stones can blacken and become cloudy with age.) Pins and clasps will be firm. Sets will bring more, for instance a bracelet with matching earrings and necklace. Particular makers will also bring more, such as Weiss, Coro, and Schiaparelli. Should a stone in a better piece be missing, there are specialists in repairing costume pieces, and your local bead store may also be able to help out.

Even if your pile of jewelry seems like junk plastic, have it looked at! Kitschy earrings, psychedelic necklaces and Bakelite, in particular, can be more valuable than you think. Bakelite is a plastic that was used to make everything from bracelets to radio knobs from about the 1940s to the 1960s. It came in a number of colors and could be carved and layered. Though the value of Bakelite has been about halved since the 1990s, it's still popular. To check for Bakelite, there are smell and rub tests that elicit a petroleum odor.. More reliable tests (should your nose fail you, as mine does) are:

1. Formula 409 Bacterial Solution. Spray a Q-Tip, then rub that on the material. The Q-Tip will turn a bright greenish-yellow if your item is Bakelite.

2. Purchase Simichrome metal polish, available for about $12 a tube online. The pinkish cream will turn dark yellow when rubbed onto Bakelite.

A self-confessed Bakelite freak has told me that the reactions are due to the patina that's built up, and not due to the Bakelite itself. Thus, if a bracelet is heavily polished or treated to bring back its original color (colors can change drastically over time from, say, purple to white), it may not react. Similarly, some colors react to one test but not the other.

Adventures in the Junk Trade: Biker Chic

When Mona, a large young gal schlepping boxes of junky bits, showed up with ... more boxes of junky bits from her deceased father's storage lockers, I braced myself. The first time she came in, I'd spent about an hour sorting mostly chaff from a few barely sellable nicknacks, pocket knives, and necklaces. Her story was touching, though, and I wanted to help her. Her dad had been a Vietnam vet who abandoned his wife and kids and spent the remainder of his life roaming from one place to another, stashing things in lockers. Mona was getting to know him solely through the stuff he'd left behind.

It happened to be a slow day when she showed up again, and I didn't mind taking the time to sift through the junk. Out of four or five cardboard boxes I put aside $25 worth of little items, including a couple of brass men's rings, each featuring a skull and crossbones. Their punky look was cool, and I wouldn't have any problem selling them at $18 apiece or so. A few days after she left, I took a look on Ebay... and found that they were "Mexican biker rings," quite popular and valued at about $130 each! I was happy when she came back in and I could share the good news about her small pot of gold among the trash!

Tips for Cleaning Jewelry

As with most other items, jewelry will sell better when it's clean. I never use silver polish, though, as it gets between stones and is difficult to remove. A better method is to soak jewelry in Polident cleaner to loosen any grunge, then use a soft toothbrush to finish.

Use a rouge cloth for removing tarnish and smudges, and for brightening up the surface. These are flannel squares infused with a polishing agent – they don't harm the silver. (Available from jewelry-supply companies and online.)

You should never use the liquid-dip polishes that take off all the tarnish. Even if you prefer silver shiny, as I do, the natural patina of aged silver, even when polished, is far more attractive than the garish sheen of stripped metal.

Should Silver/Brass/Copper Be Polished?

If you're keeping the item, there's no right or wrong. If you plan to sell it, don't polish it. Let the buyer decide.

CHAPTER 10: HOLDING A GARAGE SALE:

THE GOOD, THE BAD, THE REALLY UGLY!

Last summer a young guy showed up in my store asking me to look at a creamer he'd just bought at a garage sale. A quick glance told me it was a pot-metal piece from 100 years ago or so – common hotel ware, not valuable. When he put it on the counter, though, it was another story. He also had the sugar bowl to go with it... and both were heavy and marked "sterling"! He'd paid $10 for the set just that morning. When I weighed them for him, the silver value alone was in the $400 range, and because they were a lovely chased Victorian pair, they'd surely sell for far more than that. As you're smart enough to read this book, I have no doubt that you won't be the poor sap that mistakenly tosses solid silver into a junk box!

Garage sales can be fun... and also a great deal of work, sometimes worth the effort and sometimes not. Most of you have held them, I'm guessing, but here are some tips:

- ✓ Start advertising your sale several days ahead of when it starts by posting on Craigslist and any other free classified ads in your area (some local papers offer them for free).

- ✓ Post signs the night or two before at major intersections, using bright paper, big arrows, and large letters that can be seen by drivers without slowing down. Use the same color paper on all your signs so that drivers can follow the color alone. Be sure to include a date!

✓ Pricing each item is good practice: it saves the customer from asking; you won't have to make quick (and possibly wrong) decisions on the spur of the moment; and if you decide to put up a "1/2 Off" sign the second day, it will make more sense.

✓ Keep valuables, such as good jewelry and watches, under glass, if possible. (Lay out items in a baking pan; after removing a picture from a frame, put that framed glass on top of the box. Tape a note to the glass that says, "Ask to see.") Keep the box on your cashier's table. It's still not advisable to sell better jewelry at a sale unless there's someone to keep a constant watch.

✓ Use a fanny pack or small shoulder bag to hold the money, so that if you're moving around helping people, you won't have to keep an eye on the cash box.

✓ Don't let anyone into your house during the sale – to use the bathroom, the phone or for any other reason. I recently glanced through a book on how to "make a fortune" buying and selling stuff. The big advice the book offered was to make up any excuse at all to get into someone's garage or house in order to poke around!

✓ Have a neighbor or friend help out.

✓ See "Chapter 17: Selling Strategies"

The Upside:

■ Getting rid of junk: priceless

■ All the profit is yours

- Items you thought you'd have to give away can make you some money

The Downside:

- It can be days of work organizing, tagging, etc.

- You'll have stuff left over that you still have to deal with

- Cheapskates'll haggle with you till you want to slap them silly. Go ahead! You have my full permission!

Costs:

Financial: Expenses for markers, signs, tape, cookies to bribe the neighborhood kids to "Stop playing 'Red Rover' with Grandma's wheelchair, dammit!"

Time for: Stapling signs to telephone poles (also for heading to the local ER to have staple removed from thumb), slapping high prices on junk that should go straight to Goodwill anyway, setting up tables, putting out items, making lemonade so you don't die of thirst out there in the desert of your driveway

Guilt for: selling musical snow globe that holds a unicorn standing in a blizzard of glitter while it plays "How Great Thou Art." After all, your 45-YEAR-OLD sister sent it to you all the way from Arizona! FOR-TEE-FIVE. Does she not know better? (Really, she ought ta cut out the vino-with-Jeopardy habit.)

- More grief, when she shows up – surprise! – from Arizona, finds her lonely unicorn broiling amongst the garage sale detritus and smashes it on the neighbor's driveway.

- More grief re: cops. See above.

- Expenses and explanations for: bail. Also, plane ticket to Arizona.

CHAPTER 11: SELLING AT ANTIQUE SHOWS AND FLEA MARKETS

Adventures in the Junk Trade: Miss Bossy Boots

A bossy dame just left my shop, huffing and puffing that the shop down the street, the one that takes vintage clothes, well!, they only offered her $4 for a dress that she just knows is was worth at least $45! Well!

This lady – we'll call her Miss Bossy – had come in to ask advice about how to sell her mother-in-law's gigantic estate of purses, hats, and other accessories. The MIL had been a Southern preacher's wife and dressed the part all through the '50s and '60s, and so, of course, the goods were ... very good and so, of course, Miss Bossy should earn a bundle from them! Bossy Boots told me that she'd tried selling a few racks of the suits and dresses at Portland's recent Big Garage Sale, which involved a few dozen dealers in a convention hall. She was shocked that no one had been interested in paying the mere $45 per dress she was asking. Hmmm, I thought. She also told me that she'd purposely retired from her job early so that she wouldn't have to learn how to use a computer. Uh oh! At the library she'd looked up the value of her dad's old pop guns in a book and found that they were worth between $1,000 and $1,500. Okydoke, let's see how that works!

She needed help! When I explained that with "garage sale" as the name of the event, shoppers would be expecting ... let's see... garage sale prices, she was taken aback. Really aback! But at the sale, she complained, the guy across the aisle from her had sold car parts for big prices and he just about sold out! When I told her it sounded like he understood the market, she started to get it. At a higher-end event, I explained, she'd be in the right place to offer her desirable vintage clothes for ever-more desirable prices because collectors come to those shows specifically to find choice items that they'd rarely find at a garage sale.

That she'd done research using out-of-date materials written even a few years ago had steered her into a bog of disappointment (the word "recession" apparently meant little to her, and as she described the ma-in-law's huge house and worldly goods I got the picture that her view of money was a bit skewed). She didn't know how to navigate on Ebay and "Anyway," she asked, "Isn't Ebay saturated?" It was something she'd probably heard from a whiny girlfriend. True, Ebay isn't perfect, but as I told her, it's a great place for selling that one desirable item (see "Chapter 13: Selling on Ebay")... or a whole closetful of vintage clothes.

<u>The Latest Thing</u> There's a range of antique shows, from the most flea-bitten of flea markets to the highest end of New York extravagance. A newer sort of show is the collective, where groups of friends, crafty folks, or dealers get together to share costs. A recent trend is mixing vintage items with craft offerings. These can be fun, country sort of outings... or bad mashups of junky goods and bad crafts. These are probably not where you want to seriously sell, but I steal my best ideas at from the creative people who do!

<u>Flea Market vs. Swap Meet</u>

Flea markets can be indoors or out, weekends only or ongoing throughout the week. Here on the West Coast, *flea market* and *swap meet* may mean the same thing... or not. Generally, a swap meet offers new, cheap goods such as tennis shoes, out-of-date canned goods, and novelty keychains while a flea market is all about the cats prowling for vintage loot.

At the Starlite Drive-In in Tacoma, the swap meet happens daily all week, with the bigger kahuna – including junk dealers – taking place on Sunday. The show's an odd mix of produce, vintage stuff, and newer merchandise. In Los Angeles, a swap meet might be a cultural mélange of Latino food, music, and discount items. And just to confuse things, here in Portland there's a yearly auto swap meet that includes booths of non-auto-related vintage treasures and jewelry.

Well, you'll figure it out with a visit, which is the best way for you to decide where you want to sell your things, anyway. Be smarter than Miss Bossy by doing a little reconnaissance beforehand. Googling "flea market" should turn up at least one venue in your area

How To Sell at a Flea Market or Antique Show

Visit the venues to see which market might suit your items best and offer the most positive experience for you. Talk to the dealers, all of whom have been in your second-hand shoes.

To consider as you decide where you want to sell:

- Find out not only how much it costs, but who the usual shopper is. Is it $12 a table (or space) or $45? Is the higher cost worth it in terms of getting bigger crowds with fatter wallets? Are the customers you see there likely buyers of your items? (For instance, selling antique Louis Vuitton bags at the Funky Junk Bash might not work.)

- What's included in the cost? Portland offers a well-attended monthly show in a hotel conference center where the tables and chairs are included, as are tablecloths, free coffee and doughnuts (!) and parking for only $20 per 8-foot table. The surroundings are utterly civilized and so are the clientele.

At the other end of the teeter-totter is a seedier venue, an urban lodge hall and its parking lot, where outdoor spaces go for not much at all, but nothing's included. I don't mind being around guys who show up dirty from scrapping metal and cleaning out houses – they generally bring interesting things to sell and don't mind bargaining – but there's no question that the milieu isn't for everyone. For sale: one mummified cat under glass, seen there last summer. It's usual for banged-up box trucks to pull up and dump loads of storage-unit proceeds, most of which is unappealing. And there's no doubt that shady deals go on. I was lucky to be far across the parking lot the day an illegal gun sale went bad when the dealer accidentally fired the weapon. If colorful characters aren't your thing; if you don't want to sell in a dusty parking lot; this wouldn't be the show for you!

A metro area will host numerous flea markets. In L.A., for instance, you can shop and sell in everything from a lovely setting in the sea breeze of Santa Monica to the huge and sweltering Rose Bowl Flea Market in Pasadena. But large or small, crummy or classy, selling at a flea market means tagging and packing everything, getting up early, and you'll probably want to bring your own food & drinks to save your hard-earned money. To consider:

> Can you reserve a spot or do you have to take a chance? In my experience, it's possible at most flea markets to reserve a spot in advance. The alternative is to show up, wait in line, and hope you can be accommodated. This is just no fun if it happens to be five in the morning and you're desperate to sell.

> How easy is load-in? At most outdoor shows you can park where you sell, making unpacking easy. For indoor shows, though, you'll have to schlep your boxes in. Does the venue offer dollies? (Many do.) If not, you may have to provide your own if you don't want to take a dozen trips to your car.

> What about the weather? Will you need a pop-up canopy to keep the sun or possible showers off?

> ➤ Other considerations are: A) tables, chairs, and table covers. Find out if they're available, free or for a fee. B) your selling location within the market: are you allowed to choose it? Often, sellers with seniority have more choice. C) the refund policy should you need to cancel or reschedule, or if the show gets rained out.

Flea Market/Antique Show To-Do List

➔ Reserve space

➔ Tag items and pack boxes and car ahead of time

➔ Bring tables, chairs, and pop-up canopy or stand-alone umbrella if necessary

➔ Get plenty of small bills, a calculator (or smart phone), a receipt pad, and a small change bag/purse/fanny pack that you can't lose and that can't be easily stolen. I use a compact traveler's shoulder bag that has several zip compartments to keep both big and small bills in and that'll also hold a pen and paper. If you want to take credit card sales, the Square is cheap and easy to use.

➔ A show kit is a good idea: a couple of pieces of paper (for signs), tape, scissors, pens, and extra tags, for starters. (Mine also includes antacid and aspirin.)

➔ Bring all those plastic bags that have been multiplying under the sink.

➔ Bring food, and a cooler if it's going to be a long, hot, day.

The Upside:

• No long-term commitment

• At a show where tables/chairs are provided, you won't have much invested but your time

- No advertising necessary

- Meeting interesting people! I have flea-market friends now that have stayed friends for years.

- People often want to know about what they're buying: if you enjoy relaying the history of your merchandise, have fun!

The Downside:

- It's a whole lot of work, especially if you're on your own.

- If you're at an outdoor show, a blizzard or heat wave can really spoil the fun

- Repacking the unsold items after a long day can be disheartening...especially since *you still have them!*

- Other dealers can occasionally be rude, strange or just bothersome. (No, I really don't want to hear about your gall stones!) And it's just bad form to moon them. After all, they're your new neighbors, and you have to live with them at least for that one day.

- If the customers don't turn out, you're sunk no matter how great your stuff is.

- Watching strangers paw your grandmother's favorite sweaters can be disturbing and can certainly add to any remorse you might feel about selling her things.

- You may have to buy or borrow tables, a folding chair and canopy. Also, quite possibly, a bottle of gin.

- You'll need a big enough vehicle to carry a load of boxes

- In most cases, you're stuck once you set up: it may be physically impossible to get your car out or highly uncool to pack up early should you feel the need to quickly hop a cruise ship to Bermuda. Though who could blame you? Honestly.

Costs

Financial: Generally $10-$50 per day, depending on the venue and the amount of space you're renting; boxes, paper, tags, markers

Emotional: It can be a high to watch a customer get excited about Pop's old fishing reel! *How great that it's going to someone who appreciates it and will use it!* But it can also be a real bummer to hear the super-hip couple discuss tearing the pages out of Mom's old birding book in order to decoupage the garbage can.

Baggage: Certainly, if the items are half-decent, the prices are low, and the crowd is half drunk (har har) at least some items will sell, and possibly a lot. But others won't, and the problem of disposing of them will still be there. Also, if the sale is successful and you have a good time, you may turn into a junk junkie, seeking out even *more* stuff to sell when the big idea is to *stop the madness!*

Time: Hours tagging and packing prior to the show, a day at the show, unloading afterward, and re-storing. Then: soaking in a hot bath, and time on the phone making your best friend feel guilty for not helping you. Enjoy!

Selling at Antique Shows

Flea market on steroids, anyone? You've most likely been to one… and wondered what the hell you were thinking coming to this overcrowded, overpriced, overwhelming show! They can feel that way. Antique shows are generally kicked up a notch or nine from flea markets: the venues are better, the merchandise is more expensive, and the stakes are generally higher for the dealer.

Differences between antique shows and flea markets are many:

- A particular antique show may happen only once or a few times a year

- It's sometimes necessary to reserve even months in advance to sell at an antiques show

- Shows usually span a few days or a weekend-plus

- The costs to sell at antiques shows can be …. crazy! The Portland Antiques Expo, a two-day show with an additional day for early-bird buyers, charges (as I write this) $240 for an empty 10 x 10 space. If you want tables, chairs, electricity, a display case, backdrop or carpet, it'll cost more. And while the expense may seem ridiculous, the Expo, as it's fondly called, is one of the biggest shows on the West Coast: thousands of customers come to each show, and dealers generally leave with thousands in their happy little pockets. If you don't mind the work and the considerable time spent, a show like this may well be a good choice for reaching the most customers in the least time, all of them clearly willing to spend a few bucks (or more).

While it probably won't cost more than a couple dollars for entrance to a flea market, antiques shows may charge a lot; for instance at the Expo, early-bird entrance is $30 for Friday, when dealers set up, and $8 or so for the two weekend days. Parking is also in the $7 range, so before anyone sets foot in your booth, they've already shelled out quite a bit. This means that your customer base is either well-enough off … or entirely broke!

Larger cities host specialized shows for Modernism, fine art, glass, paper ephemera, etc. Mostly you'll find professional dealers at these, but there's no reason you, the amateur, also can't sell Uncle Fred's military memorabilia or Grandma's French dolls. Even just browsing these shows will provide some valuable information about your things.

CHAPTER 12: HOW TO SELL YOUR THINGS TO AN ANTIQUE STORE

Yes, they do! Antique stores want to buy your good junk! Seems obvious now, but back in my happy hoarder's life, I felt too intimidated to approach any resale shop about buying my stuff. Even though I knew I was good at finding things they might want, I was chicken to bother them and had no idea how to. Now that I own a store myself, the answer is... yes, they're interested! Here's how to and how *not* to deal with an antiques store.

First, determine if what you have is appropriate for an antiques store. Clock from the 1820s? Check! (Although not all antiques stores want clocks.) Mink stole from the 1950s? Try a vintage clothing store. Kermit the Frog puppet from the 1970s? A collectibles or vintage toy store would be a good bet. (If you have a lot of everything, most antique dealers would be happy to stop by your home and buy things... but that'll still leave you with leftovers.)

Depending on the size of city you live in, you may want to call around to see which stores'll be interested in your item. Let's say it's a Victrola. If you live in a larger city, a simple Google search may turn up antiques stores that focus on music. If not, I would highly recommend visiting stores that you think might be good possibilities. There's nothing more annoying to me, the buyer, than a potential seller setting one foot inside my store and asking what kinds of things I buy, when a simple jog around the aisles would *show* him what I buy. It pays to do a little research. Stating to the owner, "I've noticed you have sheet music, so I wonder…" is far more impressive to me than, "I've tried six stores already – you want an old record player?" While your goal isn't, of course, to impress the owner, making her cranky and out-of-sorts isn't a good idea when you'd like her to fork over piles of cash and take you seriously.

Once you've settled on a particular store, call to see if they're interested, and whether you need an appointment. If they say, "Just bring it in any time," ask when their slowest times are so that you don't end up waiting ages as customers are served.

If you're a thief or drug addict, first, go pay for this book; second, I won't believe you when you tell me it's Grandma's Victrola. If I think the item is stolen I might call the cops, but regardless, I have a "picker's oath" for every seller to sign swearing the item is theirs, and listing their driver's license info. So bring some ID no matter how upright and outta sight you might be. I and other dealers ask for this in order to protect ourselves if someone should claim that the Victrola was stolen from him. (And in some states every item has to be logged and the list sent to the police, as with pawn shops.)

It's not nice to hit one store after the other looking for free appraisals…especially if you present yourself as someone who wants to sell. Many dealers, myself included, may make an offer that expires the minute you step out the door. If you decide to see who'll offer the most for that Victrola, be honest that that's what you're doing, but it would probably pay higher dividends to take the item to a legitimate auction rather than alienate potential buyers of future goodies.

Antique dealers will generally pay you a third to half of what they'll ask for the item. Thus, if through your research you've found that Victrolas are generally priced at around $125, you might expect to get $50-$75. It doesn't pay to be offended by this practice, as the dealer is taking a risk, giving the item shelf space, and spending a lot on overhead such as advertising and rent. If the Victrola needs a lot of cleaning or repair work done, expect much less.

Unless the dealer/bastard says, "Take it or leave it," you're free to negotiate – it shouldn't offend a dealer who does that himself when buying. If you're offered a measly $40 for the Victrola, make a counter-offer and give reasons, if you have them, as to why your item is worth that much. And always remember: you're free to walk away. I often feel that sellers feel pressured (not by me, necessarily, but by whatever circumstances are demanding cash) and will unwisely settle for less than what they want. If I can only offer $20 for that Victrola, it might be that that's all I can afford as a dealer at the moment. The seller, rather than making a pruney face and blinking back tears, can literally take the Victrola off the table and hope that the next dealer's a little more flush.

Adventures in the Junk Trade: The Hard Couple

The couple couldn't have looked any more worried. The woman was pale, colored peach from her hair to her nails, timid and ridiculously grateful even that I'd greeted her. He was a tall man with chopped black hair storm-fashioned into knives. The lines in his 50+ face seemed to have been carved into soft flesh with a dull knife, leaving dark criss-crossing under his darker eyes. He looked like a killer – George Clooney past his prime, on a bad day, and pushed sideways into the gutter without a scream. There he lay, with his eyes on me. Would I like to buy a box of doorknobs? How 'bout a light fixture? It wasn't till after they'd left on that third visit that I guessed the sad couple had gone around their house – I pictured a leaning farmhouse – from bedroom door to bathroom door, removing the knobs.

I imagined they lived in empty rooms now: no carpets, no TV, no bowls, no chairs, no knobs. I wondered if he beat her. But all on his mind at the moment was selling me junk.

The first day, she had come alone and offered a sheaf of old book illustrations including a Puritan-looking woman with pleading eyes, a lot like she herself looked. I bought two out of 10 or so. I didn't have any use for them, really, but the lady was ever-so-thankful for the crummy $5 bill. It was one of those buys that made me feel terrible for the entire human race and perfectly rotten to have a lunch bag full of food and a store filled with spendy, useless stuff. Here was a perfectly decent woman reduced to cutting pictures out of books.

The two of them showed up the next day – a day at the store in which I made $4.50 on postcards and nothing else – with boxes carefully packed with a dozen sets of salt & pepper shakers. Maybe they were from tabletops at Denny's. Maybe they'd actually collected generic shakers of plain glass and plated tops. I bought the two less-usual sets: ceramic turkeys and pink plastic nothings from the 1950s. "That's it"? he asked. "How 'bout the teapot? I bought it for her in the '90s. It's in perfect condition."

It was bunny-and-baby-bunny shaped. Bunnies wearing floppy hats and dresses, made in China.

"It's going for $175 on Ebay."

I told him I could give him 20. He flinched. I looked it up online. He was right, and I told him so, but I knew it would sit in my shop forever and I had too much stuff already to deal with. I suggested he sell it himself on Ebay. "Too much trouble," he said.

He looked to her: "What do you wanna do?"

She fretted. He'd given it to her. I should have said no, but I was drawn by guilt to up the ante, at the same time hating the thing and hoping she'd refuse the money at all costs. "I don't think you should sell it," I said as kindly as I could – moved by and impatient with the inner drama playing out in her cringes and finger-twisting. "If it's too painful to lose it, you should keep it." He didn't seem to care if she sold it. And she was clearly readying to reach through that inferno of emotions and sear her hand plucking that twenty dollar bill from me.

"Twenty five," I said. "Sorry, that's all I can do."

They took their money out the door. And the next day I knocked the bunny's head off accidentally, busting its ears. Justice was done. A huge relief.

Getting a Clue, Part II

Which gets us to research: it's important to both buyer and seller – whether you have a high-end item or a bunch of junk jewelry – that you, the seller, do some research to arrive at what you want for it *before* you walk in the door of the store. It's happened more than once to me that a seller looks at me doe-eyed when I ask what they want, claiming, "I don't have a clue!" It's only after I take a lot of time assessing their items and making an offer that they gasp in horror and wail, "But Granny's crap's worth a lot more than that!"

It happened again this morning. A young gal brought in boxes of sub-thrift-store type costume jewelry, claiming she didn't have any idea what its value was; Grandma was moving in and they needed money. I sifted through it, and told her honestly that there was little of any worth there. She said her feelings weren't hurt because it was Grandma's stuff. Feeling sorry for her, out of three boxes I picked out a couple of small things, and made her a decent offer... that shocked and appalled her. And when I attempted to be patient and ask, "Well, what do you want, then? How much?" I got the same idiotic answer of "I don't have a clue." Unfortunately for her, this wore me out entirely and I booted the sweetly lip-pierced and tattooed and clueless lady out of the store. As nicely as possible, of course. So have an idea when you go in of not only what you want, but of what you might get.

If you seriously "don't have a clue," it will pay to get one. Have your item appraised, or do some online research (see "Chapter 7: Getting a Clue"). If you don't, you're going to suspect you're being taken to the cleaners no matter how fair the dealer's being with you. You'll leave with a head full of "maybe"s, as in "maybe it's really worth a lot more," and "maybe I should've taken it somewhere else." Without any idea of value you won't be able to bargain smartly... and the dealer may not want to deal with you again.

Adventures in the Junk Trade: Don't Tell!

Shhhh, it's a secret: You don't have to know anything about antiques to be an antiques dealer! The only thing required by law is a beat-up milk can (useless for just about anything), a cracked crock holding umbrellas, a random handful of old buttons, a shoebox full of Florida postcards circa 1953, and a Hot Wheels car missing one wheel. There are no quizzes, licenses or diplomas needed. (An appraiser, however, is a different cat altogether.) Don't be buffaloed by an antiques dealer who

*seems to know everything. That's my friend Jerry. He thinks he knows i̇
all, and he has a lot of friends just like him out there! But bluster does
not equal knowledge.*

*Unless a particular antiques dealer is a certified appraiser, the best he
can do is give you an educated assessment.*

Cynics Corner: To the dealer, your stuff is just more stuff (unless it's
extraordinarily desirable, rare, or unusual); if negotiations don't work
out, that's the way the silver melts: it's business. To you, though, the
items have personal history, more than monetary value, and their sale is
important. These opposing views can sometimes occasion hurt feelings,
as the seller feels that the buyer is lacking in empathy or appreciation.
In fact us antique dealers may seem like a pretty cold-hearted and
callous lot. We're not, but we may appear to be. While I hope this deal
turns out well and that you're as pleased as I am at the end, for me it's
not about sentiment, it's business. In order to keep my store running, I
need to be picky about what I buy, especially regarding condition. I've
heard "All it needs is a little _____" too many times! Your nice desk
may "only" need refinishing, cleaning, repairing, etc., but I (and most
other dealers) don't have time for projects, room in the garage, and no
extra money to buy things I can't sell. Don't be offended if I only want
one item out of 10.

Reasons a Dealer Might Not Want Your Stuff

- ◆ she already has several Victrolas

- ◆ there's no space in the store

- ◆ she just paid through the nose to have "I Heart Junk" tattooed on
  her tush, and now needs to spend her money on a softer chair

- ◆ in her neck of the woods there's no demand for Victrolas

- ◆ she's focusing on Brutalist Chic and a Victrola just doesn't fit in

Things to Watch Out for When Selling to an Antiques Store

An antiques dealer will look over your items extremely carefully (or should). She'll point out every flaw and drawback to the item. Let's say you have a Navajo silver and turquoise bracelet. After researching comparable prices on the internet and at other antique stores, you've decided it's worth about $150. Knowing that antique dealers will only pay half or so, you're ready to settle at $90. You take it to Mavis, a store owner down the street.

Mavis looks very knowledgeable and a little intimidating as she takes out her little magnifier and peers at the bracelet, turning it over, muttering. "Do you see this here?" she asks, pointing at a line that runs down the stone. "That crack hurts the value. And see how worn the setting is? That's not good. Also, you probably noticed it's not marked sterling. That's a sure sign that it's fake, made in China. It might not even be real silver, but it looks nice enough so I'll take a chance and give you twenty bucks for it."

Wow, she knows a lot!, you might think. But before deciding you're just a rube who knows nothing about Southwest jewelry, take a minute to consider what she's said. Is that really a crack or is it the way the stone is made? Shouldn't an older piece like your bracelet show some wear? While it's true that most sterling should be marked, a great deal of the jewelry handmade in the Southwest isn't marked at all. If the dealer has a question about the silver, she should test it in front of you. She should also have a scale to weigh the silver, and this, too, should be done in front of you. If she doesn't, it would be wise to question either her expertise or her honesty.

Questions to ask: Does Mavis sell anything like what you want her to buy? If not, she's most likely lacking expertise in that area. Antique dealers have their own interests, which will show in what they sell, for instance, Western items, modern furniture, or Japanese arts. Find one who sells silver if not Southwest jewelry.

For any item you believe may have significant value, it's wise to do some research before you go to sell, though an official appraisal may well eat up any profits you thought you'd get. The antique dealer may not have that particular knowledge; he may just be a cheapskate; and you'll end up more satisfied with the sale once you know how much to expect.

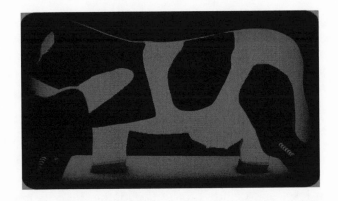

CHAPTER 13: SELLING ON EBAY AND CRAIGSLIST

I suppose the selling world can be divided into two kinds of people: those who "do Ebay," and those who don't. If you're well acquainted with Ebay, this chapter isn't for you, as you'll already have a sense of what to sell online, and how to do it. If you're *not* an Ebay person, this chapter isn't for *you*, either! You'll want to pick up an entire book on how to sell on Ebay, take a class, or skip it altogether, as it's a lot of work to learn and put into action.

This chapter, instead, is for those who know how to sell on Ebay but are unsure if it would be worth the time as far as selling off those estate items. The simple answer is: Yes. If the pieces you have to sell are antiques, desirable vintage, or collectibles, there's a market on Ebay, in fact often a better market than you'll find at an auction or antique show.

Let's say you have an antique drafting set with bone handles. You don't know the value, only that it belonged to Granddad and surely must be special as he bought it Vienna probably decades ago, and kept it in beautiful condition all these years.

I recently saw that desirable drafting set overlooked at an auction because the buyers there were hot to acquire the trendy advertising signs and modern furniture that was also up for bid. The drafting set had been put in a box lot with antique woodworking planes and the box was tucked under a table during the preview. No one looked at them except me (because I'm extra superduper smart! And also very short!) and a really old guy who needed a set of new teeth more than he needed old tools. Knowing that planes can sell for around $18 each, I flung my bidding card in the air at $25 and was the only one who wanted the stuff.

I still had no idea about the value of the drafting set, and was disheartened to see that on Ebay there were a dozen similar sets of all sizes, but none that seemed to be fetching much money. None, however, had bone handles. I set my price fairly low ($19) since I didn't have much to lose, and decided to let the market take its course: a man in Australia bought the set for upwards of $80.

There are so many variables in selling on Ebay that it's difficult to give any advice regarding pricing strategy. Should you offer the item on a Buy It Now? (Not an auction, but a set price.) Price it with a reserve? Price it low so that bidders will fight over your item and run the bid higher than if you'd set the opening bid high? I've been selling on Ebay for more than almost 15 years, and I still haven't settled on one perfect way. The following seems to work fairly well, in general:

1. Check Ebay Completed Listings to see the auction results of similar items.

2. Choose an opening bid price that you can live with. If it's under the dollar amount at which most folks are starting their auctions, you'll get more attention, and probably more bids.

3. Say *auf Wiedersehen* to that Viennese drafting set!

The Upside:

> ➤ You may find that single buyer who's been looking for that one particular item. If you're lucky you'll find quite a few, and if your price is low they'll fight to win that special thingie.

> ➤ There's little financial risk in listing an item: most listings cost under a couple of bucks, depending on Ebay's mood that day:

Sometimes it's free to add photos or it's free to list items as Buy It Now. Regardless, I rarely spend more than $1 per item regardless of discounts.

➤ The profit will be 90% yours, with 10% or so going for Ebay and Paypal fees.

➤ You can get rid of things efficiently by listing items in a lot, such as "100 rhinestone brooches," or "scrap silver" or "1950s ties."

➤ You don't have to know the value of the item you're selling if you decide to let the market set it.

The Downside:

➤ It takes time to list each item. If you have lots of things to sell, it may be utterly wasteful to spend your time taking and editing photos, writing auction listings, and packing stuff to ship.

➤ It's a huge pain any time a customer returns an item. Ebay sides with the buyer no matter what. Should a customer accidentally drop your grandma's Spode pitcher after taking it out of the box, the customer can tell you it was broken in shipping and demand her money back. If you don't refund the money, the customer can complain to Ebay and the customer will win every time. Thus, I insure every single item (or send it Priority shipping, which includes insurance), which costs more for all involved, and makes my listings less desirable to bid on.

➤ Waiting for auctions to end takes time.

➤ For high-end art or antique silver, for instance, which commands a very particular audience, you may do much better at a high-end auction where Mr. or Ms. Big Stuff goes to buy. While your Warhol may sit for $30,000 on an Ebay Buy It Now (yes, I have seen that!), at the right art auction you won't have to wait, the buyers are poised, and the setting is appropriate.

> It's always possible to sell an item for far less than you want if you take a chance on starting the bid price low. The trick is to decide before you list it what your risk should be: is it worse to end up with the item, or to sell it too cheaply?

Costs:

Time – Lots of it for taking pictures and editing them, writing each listing, answering emails from customers, waiting for listings to end, finding packing supplies and then packing each item; printing labels and dropping boxes at the post office. I anticipate about an hour per item, all told.

Money – Minimal to list an item, a bit to acquire packing supplies including marking pens, bubble wrap, boxes, etc. You can use your smart phone to take photos and list items, but for better pics (and results) you'll need a better camera.

Baggage – Selling one item at a time can be painfully slow and drawn out. Also, there are times when you may want to know who's buying that particular thing – maybe it's your mom's ring, or dad's favorite hammer. It really shouldn't matter, since you're saying goodbye to it, but hey, sometimes it *does* matter. On Ebay you'll never see the person you sell the item to, and aside from a quick email, you'll have no connection at all. If you don't want to give your "baby" up to a complete stranger who may in fact be a resale company, Ebay isn't the way to go.

Effort – Yes, you have to dedicate yourself to it.

As I write this, I have about a dozen items up for bid on Ebay. Because I purchased them at bargain rates at estate sales and flea markets, I've set the opening bid prices low. Even if they sell at that low price, then, I'm still making money – and in a sense it doesn't matter what the "worth" price is!

Selling on Craigslist

This free and freewheeling online-classified-ads site offers both huge benefits and huge disadvantages vis a vis selling estate items.

You can easily post just about anything for sale. In short, you describe your item, upload a photo or two, and bingo!, you're in business. (You can even register for a free account where you can save your listings.) The way it works is: your new ad starts at the top of the column in that category until the next ad is loaded on by the next advertiser, etc., and so by day's end your ad is way way down on the list and will continue being shoved down until it drops off entirely in a week. Hint: If you edit it, it goes back to the top, and ads are easy to relist. You can include numerous photos, and a Google map that shows your location.

For your purposes, Craigslist is great for:

- Advertising a garage sale at which low-end items will be sold

- Selling a car

- Selling appliances or furniture pieces from your driveway, yard or garage. While it would make sense to have a prospective customer come inside to see your couch, this customer could be anyone, and may have his or her eye out for smaller valuables to pilfer.

- The horror stories of selling via Craigslist are abundant, but of course there's always a risk when meeting strangers. Suffice it to say that you should not:

  - advertise any expensive items to be either sold out of your home or out of an uninhabited home (your recently deceased aunt's, for instance), which is an open invitation to squatters and thieves.

  - advertise an estate sale if the home is going to be vacant prior to the sale. Estate sale companies routinely announce the address of their sale only the night before, when they're going to have someone there to keep an eye out

- take a check

Possible solutions to the *stranger* problem:

- Should you be selling furniture via a classified ad, and you have no choice but to sell it from the house, make sure there are two people there at all times to keep an eye out.

- To sell smaller items via classified ad, arrange to meet the prospective buyer at a neutral location, such as a shopping-mall parking lot where there are plenty of people around.

The Upside:

- Items can be sold quickly

- All the profit is yours

The Downside:

- The stranger problem

- You'd be selling one item at a time

Costs:

Financial: Little to none.

Time: Minimal. You'll need a camera to upload photos.

Relief: Should the item sell quickly, you'll heave a sigh and high-five your kids. Alternately, though it doesn't take much actual work, there's a stress factor in waiting for responses and anticipating meeting up... and if it doesn't sell, you'll be back at square one.

CHAPTER 14: AN ESTATE SERVICES COMPANY CAN EASE THE BURDEN

As I mentioned in the introduction, when my mother died, my dad immediately wanted everything gone... and my sister and I were at a loss. We didn't have time, we weren't emotionally prepared, and, frankly, we "didn't have a clue" about the options for estate liquidation. Add to that the grief and shock, and the complications of other relatives and friends (at the age of 79, my newly widowed dad was suddenly a hot prospect among his many lady friends... one of whom came to my mother's celebration of life event demanding to know why he hadn't invited her!) Every sad situation has some humor in it, and cheers to you if you can glean any entertainment from your own circumstances. You certainly have my sympathy!

Looking back, an estate sale or estate auction might have been a good choice for deaccessioning furniture, dishes, and everything a family will accumulate over the years. There was lots of everything from cookbooks to antiques and smaller collectibles. An estate-services company could have taken care of the entire household – either by buying all of it (yes, there are companies that do that), or through any combination of estate sale, sending items to auction, and consigning them. However they chose to handle it, it would have been done and done! But I had no idea that such companies existed, and I wasn't aware that there were local auctions that handled everyday items. My idea of an auction was either artsy charity nights, or Christies, Sothebys ... the big national auction houses that hit the news by selling paintings fo millions.

When I phoned a couple of estate sale companies (as opposed to estate services, they merely hold sales; they don't necessarily help with other options in liquidating items, such as an auction), they seemed barely interested and wanted a guarantee of $6,000 in household goods. (I have since discovered that this isn't a hard-and-fast standard within the industry.) Unfortunately, I felt intimidated by the ladies I spoke with and my sister and I had our own sale instead. MISTAKE! We had no one watching the several doors out of the house, or keeping an eye on the individual rooms; lots of things disappeared. We didn't monitor how many people were in the house at once, and ended up with a huge crush of customers. We were in that state of grief in which nothing much matters except taking care of the business that we had to attend to: we didn't pay attention to prices, or to what was being sold. My sister and I were doing our best to be civil and not be "grabby" about things; however, the deep attachments and losses that are felt in that situation make it virtually impossible to be objective. Hire someone else! There are "living estate sales," as well, for those who are downsizing.

An estate services company can assess the value of what you have, offer advice on the best way to sell it; they can take care of all the details of that sale, from tagging to advertising; and they can leave the house "broom clean" so that you'll have little else to worry about. A larger estate services company may use a variety of tools to liquidate the household, for instance, holding an estate auction in the house itself, taking certain items or box lots to its own auction house, or selling them in other ways.

Every company, though, is different. Company A may hold estate sales only while Company B does it all. As one local estate business advertises: "From one item to entire estates, [our] team can appraise your assets and settle your estate. For the attorney, trust department or the citizen, our service is complete, professional, and confidential. Through private sales or public auctions, entire estates can be liquidated quickly, efficiently and with maximum results....We conduct professional auctions in a variety of formats, including traditional LIVE auctions, specialty auctions, and on-site auctions. We are able to provide a variety of liquidation services to meet your needs, including estate sales, tag sales, auction estimates, and appraisals."

Estate Sales

The difference between a garage sale and an estate sale is that theoretically the entire household is offered at the estate sale, from the bathroom to the basement. In reality, you will have taken out the things you want to keep (or locked them into a room) and the rest of it stays in the house for the public to pick through.

There are no rules, regulations or licenses required of those who hold estate sales or offer estate services. While there's an organization called the American Society of Estate Liquidators, which offers classes, memberships, and a code of ethics, it's not necessary to belong to it before touting yourself as an expert. Anyone can set up shop! Those running estate sales range from an inexperienced family member, to a solid estate liquidation company that's insured and bonded and may have been in business for years and years. (It's recommended that you hire a company that has both liability insurance and workman's compensation coverage.)

As a buyer I've been to dozens of sales held by a wide variety of estate liquidation companies (mostly, "company" means one person who hires helpers for each sale). I've learned who prices items too high, who's willing to haggle, and which of the local estate sale companies I can count on to price something way too low.

In all, there's one company in particular – I'll call it Big Ape Estates – that I favor as a buyer... but would never recommend to a friend who wanted her household liquidated. Why? Most items are sold extremely cheaply; for instance, coffee-table art books – beautiful glossy books that retail at $30-$60 each – go for a dollar apiece. True, the low prices mean most things will sell, but I've found bargains at Big Ape sales that would make the owner cringe – art glass and paintings and other treasures priced lower than Goodwill junk.

I was recently invited to an estate sale put on by a friend who – never mind that she doesn't know antiques from Shinola – decided to start an estate sale company to make a little extra money. She said there was a necklace I'd like that would make the 20-mile drive worthwhile. And sure enough there was, although she hadn't realized it was broken. "Well," she added, seeing my disappointment, "there's a junk-jewelry box under the counter. Maybe you'll find something there." And how! Six pair of sterling earrings, a 14K bangle and a gold necklace. "Are you sure you want to sell this stuff for this cheap?" I asked. "Yeah, of course," she said ... after all, the box was marked "50 cents each"! Even when I called her later to inform her of the gold (that I'd tested by then), she insisted that I'd found it all fair and square. I couldn't help but wonder about the owner of these things. Maybe they wouldn't know or wouldn't care much, but if I were them, I'd be unhappy. My friend was sincere in wanting to do a good job, but just didn't know enough (or have enough time) to do it right, to the loss of the owner.

A reputable estate sale company will research various items to insure they're priced correctly, though I'd guess there are very few who'll consult an appraiser, considering the expense. Thus, if there are items you consider particularly valuable, it may pay off for you to have them appraised prior to hiring the company. It might make sense then to consign them to a better auction house rather than have them go at a fire-sale price.

There are numerous ways for an estate liquidator to make you, the estate owner, unhappy, either willfully or unwittingly. Rather than recount the tales I've heard of liquidators taking advantage of their customers, it's better to recall some of the advice offered earlier in this book:

- Educate yourself about what you have (at least the pieces you believe to be the most important) by being your own appraiser or by having those items appraised prior to the estate sale. Don't count on the liquidator to know the value of every item, from an egg timer to a fishing pole.

- Do a Google search for the company. You might be surprised by what you find!

- Decide for yourself, before meeting with the liquidator, whether you'd like things priced extremely low to sell quickly, or whether you'd like to try getting more for them, at least on the first day. While the company will be setting prices, you should be able to weigh in and be listened to.

- Interview (and get blank contracts from) at least two different estate liquidators. Each should take a look at what you have, and give you a ballpark estimate of what the goods will bring.

Questions to ask the company representative:

- Are you bonded and insured?

- What do you do to advertise a sale? (A good company, for instance, will have its own email list and will post notices online and sometimes in the newspaper, as well as posting signs the day of the sale.)

- What happens to the leftovers? Some companies assure that the house will be entirely cleaned out; others charge an additional fee for it. The more established companies will have lists of dealers who buy estate leftovers to sell on their own. If this happens, you should get a percentage of that amount.

- How many employees will be at the sale?

- What sort of security is offered before and during the sale? If something's stolen, who's liable for it?

- Do you allow the client to weigh in on the prices set? To be present during the sale? (Big Ape, for instance, asks clients *not* to be at the home during the sale.)

- Do you do any research in order to price things?

- How long a sale will it be, and will items be discounted the last day?

- What sort of accounting is given at the end, and how long will it take to get it? (This should be written down)

- What happens should you change your mind about certain items and remove them from the sale? (It is, apparently, common to charge the client the 30% commission that that item would have brought at the sale.)

- Get a written list of any extra fees that may be charged

Before choosing a particular company, attend one or more of their sales. If it's disorganized, priced too low or too high, has poor security, signage and help, give them a pass. In the last year, I've found these interesting things at estate sales: a bong complete with pot residue in the bowl; a shoebox full of prescription bottles, still holding pills and still labeled with the owner's name; credit cards and driver's licenses; personal mail, including bills. Obviously, you wouldn't want these companies selling *your* stuff!

Watch to see if every item that's sold is being written down or is at least rung up through the cash register. (Often, especially on the last day of a sale, a pile of customer purchases will be bundled and sold at a discount. Still, this should be rung up and accounted for, at the least as "miscellaneous.") At the Big Ape sales, when the line for the cashier gets long, a clerk speeds things up by taking cash payments from those waiting. The money goes into her pocket. Nothing is noted. Employees are "paid" with items from the sale. It's no surprise, then, that there are complaints about Big Ape's poor business practices – a lack of accounting, little money made, etc.

Because this sale will surely be of the utmost importance to you and will likely involve a great deal of money, you might have a lawyer check out the contract.

Unfortunately, there are a multitude of ways that an unscrupulous estate sale company can take advantage, from putting a clause in the contract that allows them to buy any leftovers at 10 cents on the dollar... and then hiding items until the sale ends... to putting aside preferred customers to buy at a discount. I've also been to sales that were quite obviously "salted" by the estate company: for instance at the estate sale of a middle-income senior, complete with bad clown paintings and so-so furniture, there was a strange assortment of out-of-place Asian "antiques" including a giant gong. They'd clearly been brought in to beef up the sale, but it's unlikely that the recipient of the estate proceeds received any money from those goods.

I'm still a believer in the value of reputable estate sale companies, though, and mention the pitfalls so that you'll look for a company that serves your needs, is accountable, and follows through.

<u>The Upside of Employing an Estate-Services Company</u>

✓ The hassle is out of your hands

✓ Everything you want to be gone will be gone (if you opt for that; otherwise, you can be left with the leftovers)

The Downside of Employing an Estate-Services Company

✓ The hassle is out of your hands; if you feel that you want more control, this wouldn't be a good choice.

✓ The company will get a percentage of the take, normally around 30%; be sure to read the contract and understand all the fine print before signing.

✓ The sale won't happen immediately. It can be weeks and possibly months before you're put on the company's schedule and possibly weeks or months before you're paid.

CHAPTER 15: THE WEIRD AUCTION WORLD

Auctions can be a great way to divest yourself of all kinds of items, from the bedsteads to the wheelbarrow. There are barn auctions, tool auctions, neighborhood and high-end auctions. Got a Picasso? That can go, too!

Adventures in the Junk Trade: If These Walls Could Bid

My first experience with the weird auction world was at a charity event in Los Angeles. A nonprofit I'll call Jay's Room provided free art classes to foster kids, so it made sense that they'd hold an art auction. A well-known gallery owner donated his services as an auctioneer and a variety of local artists donated artwork. Thus, the walls of the gallery were lined with wonderful paintings, and a well-heeled crowd turned out to sip white wine and bid on new artworks to take home. Though I was barely so-so heeled, I wanted to support the friend whose event it was, and maybe even buy a piece of art.

As a colorful still life came up for bid – a can of Fanta, a dead rabbit, and a remote control on a Formica table – I watched the action from the back of the room. The auctioneer, a fiery, fat little chap, raised his hands and voice like a mad evangelist: "Who'll bid for the children?! Here's an original, uh, postmodern urban oil by Yaro Blade, you won't find another this side of the Mississippi, and who by God is gonna give *one little bid for the kids?, I said who?!" The tall guy a few rows in front of me, that's who. He raised his paddle at $25 and just kept raising it 45, 50, 75... The auctioneer looked back toward me as he had throughout, nodded and shouted, "And it's 80 in the back, do I hear one hundred?!" But I wasn't bidding and there wasn't anyone else there but me. Ohhh! The poor fellow really wanted this painting, and he wasn't going to be stopped. Sweat popped out and he grimaced like a race-car driver on a tight turn as he raised his paddle again and again. He had to have imagined that some cool cat behind him with pockets much deeper than his was silently raising a mere eyebrow over and over. Finally, at $285, with a deflated sigh, he gave up. He shook his head and dropped his paddle in his lap. "Come on now, one more time for the children," the auctioneer exhorted, but nothing doing. The hearty bidder was done and done in. The auctioneer suddenly wasn't so confident as he sputtered a "SOLD!" and moved on quickly to the next artwork.*

It was too bad for everyone – the artist's work didn't sell, the charity didn't get anything from the imaginary sale, and the would-be buyer went home disappointed.

I've heard similar stories about various auction houses: "The walls bid, the chairs bid, everything bids!" one auction-house owner told me about another local company. If you've consigned items to be sold, this might be a perversely good thing for you in the sense that you'll make more money. But a rat is a rat. Auctioneers actually hold a great deal of power once they're at the podium. I recently annoyed an auctioneer by bidding at the very last second – after he'd started to drop the hammer during a protracted bidding war between two other people. So instead of raising the next bid by the $10 increment that he had been, he raised it only $5. The previous bidder only had to bid that $5 more to get the item, and then I'd have to outbid him by $10 and so on. I found it vexing, but... *whatever.* Auctioneers at any but the largest auction houses can do what they want, really, which is part of the unpredictable game. They can refuse to recognize your bid even if you're jumping up and down on your chair. They can take one bid and call Sold! if they feel like it... or after taking your bid, wait an eternity for someone else to bid rather than let you have the item. After all, unless you're selling your items at Sotheby's or any of a number of other higher-end auction houses, you're dealing with a local yokel who's on his or her throne reining over his minions as he wishes.

A common practice at the lower-end auctions is for an auctioneer to start the bidding high – say, $75 for a chair – and if no one bids, to go *down* instead of up, knowing that eventually someone will go for it. It's not a smart practice, because the buyers know to wait until the price drops before bidding, and if I were the consignor it wouldn't make me happy to know that the auctioneer was practically giving away my things to the lowest bidder.

Before consigning to any auction house, attend an auction there to see if the auctioneer is doing his job, and whether the goods that are offered are similar in price and quality to what you have. (For example, you don't want to sell Aunt Minnie's English sterling pieces at an auction house that mostly handles box lots of household junk.) Is the auctioneer letting things go too cheaply? Does she go off on tangents, telling personal stories instead of actually selling? At a gallery-run art auction in Los Angeles I attended, the auctioneer got tired of slogging through the huge inventory of work and decided just to skip over pieces he thought no one would want. "Call out what you want to bid on," he told the audience. "Otherwise, I'll jump ahead." I imagine that there were a lot of unhappy consignors that day whose work never saw the auction block let alone made any money.

That said, I do believe most auction houses, no matter how small, try to be fair. For one thing, even country auctions miles from anywhere can be broadcast live over the internet through Proxibid, Auction Zip or another online venue, making them subject to at least a small amount of scrutiny. Auction results are posted and auctions can be viewed and heard in real time. If you're considering a particular auction house, you can check out one of their auctions without leaving your home.

What to consider when deciding on an auction house:

- ✓ What kind of items do they sell?

- ✓ Are their auctions held online live? (IE, on Auction Zip, Proxibid, LiveAuctioneer, etc.?) If not, that auction house may not generate the number of bidders and higher prices that might be otherwise had.

- ✓ Can you request a reserve (the lowest price at which you'll sell the item)? If not, what price would be the opening bid price for your tuba/necklace/dishwasher? Will you be unhappy if the item sells no higher than that? (Typical opening bids at lower-end auctions range from $10 to $45. An item may sell for a great deal more, but it can also sell for the measly price at which it opens.)

- ✓ What's the reputation of that auction house? Do a Google search, check references, and look at the auction results they've gained (the online bidding sites show completed auctions).

- ✓ How much will you have to pay for a seller's commission? Read their terms and apply them to a possible auction. Not so long ago, for instance, I took six cookie jars to a local auction to be sold in one lot. I'd had them in my store for months, and no one showed any interest. Rather than donate them or sell them at a flea market, I hoped that at the auction, sold together, they'd bring a little more. But – oh, dang! – they sold for only $25, and the commission on that amount was 50%! Considering the bother of packing them and taking them there... (As at most auctions, the commission rates are variable depending on how much the item sells for.)

- ✓ Ask what other charges you may be liable for. The larger auctions may charge for storage, handling, insurance, restoration, photography, advertising and more.

The Upside of Selling at Auction

- With luck, your items will sell and you'll make some money

- The audience is there to buy and should have plenty of time to examine your things either through the auction catalog or during the auction preview, when customers can check out the goods in person

- You can attend the auction (or follow it live online in most cases) and see for yourself what happens

The Downside of Selling at Auction

- It's possible your item doesn't sell

- Selling one item at a time can be tedious

- The high-end auction house that's agreed to consign your jade tiger may only host auctions for Asian art a few times a year. It can also take weeks to get paid. No auction is immediate, not even the local ones.

- You're responsible for getting your things to the auction house, whether it's hauling a single chair to Bubble's Bid-o-Rama down the block or shipping a fragile chandelier across the country. Gas and postage add up, so you'll have to consider whether the gamble (will the item make enough to justify all the work you're going to?) is a good one. If the item doesn't sell, you'll also be responsible for getting it back to your place.

How Selling at Auction Works

Major Auction Houses:

All the large auction houses, such as Bonham's, Sotheby's, Christie's, Skinner, and Swann, have websites that offer an overview of the areas in which they specialize, catalogs of upcoming auctions, and results of past auctions. They also have ready information on how to consign an item for auction, but often don't offer obvious information on what their rates are. (See info below on charges.) If you have a piece that you'd like to consign, you can generally email photos and information on it to the auction house, which will then let you know whether they're interested in taking it for consignment and will provide you with an auction estimate at no charge. This can take days to... never.

In practice, I've had both good and bad experiences in offering items to different auction houses. The reality seems to be that if they're not interested, they may just forget about you altogether. It's annoying and a big waste of time. Thus, there's nothing at all wrong with offering your tiger to several auction houses simultaneously. At the least it'll tell you who's responsive and which auction house to skip the next time around; at best, more than one auction house will want to consign the tiger, and you can compare the estimates you're given.

The auction house arrives at its estimate by looking at past auction results of comparable items. Let's say they estimate your tiger at $1,200. If the desirability of jade tigers has shot up since the last jade tiger sold, you may be in for an unexpected windfall of even thousands of dollars. Likewise, if the buyers of jade tigers have moved on to collecting silver ducks, well, you might be out of luck.

The commission the auction house takes will vary depending on how much the item sells for, usually from 10% to 30%. The higher price at which the item sells, the lower the commission. The buyer also pays a commission, ranging from about 10% to 18% of the final price of the item.

Some larger houses hold live evaluation events at which they'll give you an informal valuation, and possibly a ballpark auction estimate (or let you know your item isn't worthy!). (Dates will be listed on their web sites.) It's important not to mistake these *Roadshow*-style look-sees for actual appraisals. The auction house is seeking out inventory, and that's all. They're not offering evaluations as a public service, and won't give you anything like the time or discourse that *Antiques Roadshow* does.

If they're interested in selling your treasure, they'll likely offer you an estimate of what they think your tiger will bring, and you'll have the choice of letting them take the item... or not (you are under no obligation).

In my experience, these events can be fun, and I've learned a thing or two. Such as: clown art on velvet? Probably not! In Los Angeles I stood in a long line next to a soap opera actor I'd watched as a teenager, a very chatty man, and that experience ended up being worth a lot more than the painting I'd taken to have looked at!

Mid-range and Smaller Auction Houses:

These, too, will likely have websites with information about upcoming auctions, but consigning items to them will entail merely talking with them about what you have, then signing a contract when you drop off the item.

While a great many local houses don't specialize in any one type of item, others may handle only folk art, Indian crafts, autographs, etc. It may be worth your while to find the auction house that's looking for jade tigers, English clocks, or vintage photographs.

Costs of Selling at Auction

Money: Postage for shipping items, gas for delivering and retrieving things; commission fees should the item sell; possible miscellaneous fees that you may be charged whether your item sells or not

Time: For research, contacting auction houses and submitting info (or showing items), then for waiting. It can be a long process!

CHAPTER 16: DONATE FOR GOODNESS SAKE!

In addition to the Salvation Army, Goodwill and St. Vincent de Paul, there are lots of places to donate goods of all types. Here are just a few that aren't so obvious:

◆ Most public schools in colder climates are happy to receive coats, boots, gloves, even socks to give to kids who need them

◆ The canned and dry goods left in Aunt Jane's cupboards will be more than welcomed by any food bank or homeless shelter

◆ Homeless shelters differ in their needs, but blankets, jackets and sometimes household goods and furniture can often be distributed among those in need

◆ Camping items and sports equipment might be shared with a Campfire or scouting group

◆ Antiques, collectibles and artwork may be welcomed as items in charity auctions of all kinds. Animal-themed items might go to a pet shelter

◆ Books can be donated to senior centers, veteran's groups, and your local library

◆ Oddball craft items will most likely be welcomed by scouting troops, senior centers, and schools

◆ Sports items can go to after-school groups, the Y, or local daycares

◆ And, of course, Habitat for Humanity takes construction cast-offs, tools, paint, windows and everything else building related, including vintage fixtures, old tiles, etc.

Check with an estate lawyer to see what sort of documentation you need for your tax purposes.

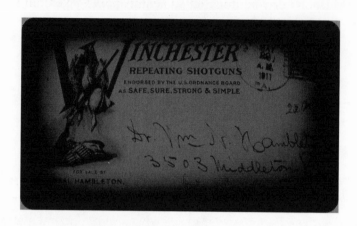

Chapter 17: Sales Strategies

Unless you sell at a high-end auction or hire an estate sale company, you'll have to choose a pricing strategy. I have no doubt that many a Harvard MBA thesis has been written about retailing, but here's the view from a dealer in the trenches. (Pass me that mustard gas, eh, Shorty?)

Perhaps when the economy was *go-go-go,* pricing items at the high end paid off. As I write this, though, the economy is not so good and hasn't been for years. People will pay a fair price and sometimes – when they're splurging at a ritzy show or if they're on vacation and blowing out some dough – a little more. But generally they want good value for their buck. So here are the choices as I see them:

Garage Sale You have little time to sell, so you have little choice: Price everything as cheaply as you can bear to see it go. No *book value, market value,* or any other value besides: It's Got To Go value! If it's going to hurt to see Aunt Coco's mink stole sell for $20 or less, save it or sell it differently. Be prepared to entertain insulting offers and to bargain back. And please, for hecksake, do not utter the words too often pronounced at junk sales, "Well, on Ebay it goes for…"! Yikes. If you want the Ebay price, best to sell it on Ebay.

<u>Flea Markets and Antique Shows</u> By this point, you should have a good idea of the market value of your things, either by being your own appraiser or by having things appraised. There are several ways to go:

- High to Low: Let's say your Nippon chocolate pot has a value of between $40 and $60, as you've found on Ebay. It's in excellent condition, has a lot of visual appeal, and is currently in vogue. You like it but it has to go, as it takes up a lot of space and isn't to your taste. You might try pricing it at the higher end, and then lower the price as the show goes on. The risk is that someone who might have purchased it at $35 has already left the show by the time you mark the pot down. If you price things this way, you're likely to be left with quite a few items unsold. If that's preferable to you than selling things cheaper, this would be the way to go. For an entire booth of things, putting up a sign at two o'clock announcing 50% off is like catnip to a cageful of hungry tigers. Watch out!

- The One Price strategy, also great for garage sales: You might have a $1 table, a $5 table and a $10 table. You can mark each item with a colored dot, you don't have to bargain, and it's fun for the buyer to find sweet deals. I've seen $5 booths even at expensive antique shows when dealers are selling off their extra stuff or going out of business. Eezy peezy! More hungry tigers! The upside? Ready cash and empty boxes. The downside? It's difficult not to have regrets when you're selling that choice chocolate pot for only $10. I recently had a sale like that, and decided to try selling one of the leftover vases online. It was hand painted, Chinese export ware (late 1800s), large and in perfect condition. It hadn't sold at either my store, for $24, or on the $10 table at a smalltown flea market. But it *did* sell on Ebay... for $44! (And it's possible it would have sold at a higher end auction for even more.) That knowledgeable buyer was out there.

- The Go Low approach: As these are things that you don'
want to hang onto; you're more eager to shed them than to
make a bundle of dough; and you don't want to lug anything
back home, price everything at 25% to 40% below the
market value you've come up with. The dealers won't leave
you alone! Word gets around quickly that "Hey, that booth
over there is blowing things out!" If you don't want to dicker
further on things, you can gently remind would-be buyers
that, "Sorry, I've already priced everything just as low as I
can... but if you buy more than fifty bucks worth I can give
you another 10% off." Being sympathetic and working with
customers can make a world of difference.

- The Stick-to-Your Guns strategy: I see this quite a bit at
antiques sales and it always annoys me: the dealer has
looked at New York auction results and priced his items to
match, never mind that he's selling at a dusty little flea
market. By God, he's going to $65 for that rusty vintage
tricycle no matter what because that's what it's worth! Well,
good luck to him, and good luck to you if you use this
approach. You'll end up with a garage stuffed with
"valuable" items that no one will buy! Better to be a bit
flexible; remember that the idea is to *sell*, not to hang onto;
and let things go.

You've been to that garage sale, I'm sure, where everything is priced as
if the driveway is a chi-chi antique store in NYC! *Get real!*, you want
to say to the homeowner – you know, the gal standing there in flip-flops
and shorts? She's got an attitude that says, *Don't touch my incredible,
valuable junk,* and I'm happy to oblige. I have a hard time keeping my
trap shut, though, and my partner, Frank, kind soul that he is, is ever
dragging me by the elbow back to the car as I'm muttering under my
breath, "Can you believe those crazy prices?!"

"Anything will sell," a dealer friend likes to say, "if it's priced low
enough." It goes to the point that selling quickly means selling more

cheaply. The lower the price, the faster it will go, and if you only have a one-day garage at which to sell things...

There are some odd exceptions to this rule, and one is that perception means a lot in this business. In other words, the monetary value you place on your item may translate to the material value the buyer places on it. For example, I have a display case in my store with nicer pottery in it: Van Briggle, and Rookwood, and I had a Hull vase that I wasn't nuts about. It had come in a box lot, and I didn't mind selling it cheaply to make room for pieces I enjoyed more. And so I priced it at about half of the usual going rate for that vase, $35 rather than $75 or higher. I learned a lesson when, twice in a month, customers asked what was wrong with it. When I said "Nothing," they objected. "There *has* to be something wrong with it!" a lady shrieked to her husband. When I assured her it was a good piece, that I'd purchased it and priced it myself, she became utterly deflated. "No," she told hubby, "I really don't want to buy it." My guess was that she had paid considerably more for one herself – which she treasured as a valuable collectible – and now it just seemed cheap. (I later repriced it higher and sold it.) It's unlikely, though, that this exception would apply at a garage sale, where that same $35 would simply seem like a bargain to the lady, a great deal on a $75 vase!

Adventures in the Junk Trade: Holding Things Dear

If you're selling things you don't care much for and just want to get rid of, it's likely you won't object to selling them cheaply. If you're anything like my new pal Darren, though, a hoarder at heart whose every item is a treasure, you may be in trouble when it comes time to sell.

It finally came out: the key to Darren's incredible collection of 1920s lamps, high-end glass vases, and Asian tchotchkes was a rather large inheritance of some $600,000 he'd gotten several years ago. Rather than take up the offer to invest it in what's now a booming shopping center, he chose to spend it all on beautiful, remarkable items. A houseful of them. And now he's broke. His house is in foreclosure. A few months ago he hired an estate sale gal to sell much of it, but the

*prices she was tagging things with were, he believed, ridiculously low
and just making him crazy. So at night he'd creep back into the house
snatch things from the tables and pack them carefully into plastic bins.*

*The estate sale was my introduction to his wild collection, and his wilder
prices. I bought two little things at that sale – an Art Nouveau fairy
whose wings were broken, and an ugly wooden cigarette box painted
with a Viking ship. Why did I buy it? Because the sale was crowded, and
I'm short. I had to fight my way through a tall, stifling throng of dealers
– like a little salmon shoving herself upstream -- and once I grabbed
that goddam box I was Not! Going! To let! GO! Not no-how, no matter
how ugly it was! (Childish, yes!) And I couldn't afford anything else. It's
silly, but it happens that you want to go home with a treasure of some
sort, even if it's just a battle bruise!*

*The next week, Darren, a middle-aged, mild-mannered Clark Kent,
introduced himself to me in my store and invited me to come shop solo
through what was left of this things. But he just can't let go. He spent a
lot of money and he wants a lot of money. His stuff is worth far more to
him than cash. And as I poke through piles of vases and pictures, I can't
bring myself to tell him he's out of his mind asking what he's asking.
Instead I plead poormouth, I compliment his good taste, I fairly drool
over the even more astonishing items that aren't for sale: a metal lamp
in the shape of a Venetian boat, the light shining from behind through
stained pearly glass like a huge moon. Eventually he goes down a bit
and I spend more than I should on a 1920s floor lamp with its original
purple fringe shade; a large porcelain Siam couple painted beautifully
and doing double duty as lamps; and a few small vases.*

*That was several months ago. Now Darren's getting more desperate,
knowing he'll be booted out of his house any day. He offers woodblock
prints on Craigslist for $750. No dice. He invites me again to his house,
and I go and buy quickly without lollygagging and oohing and ahhing
as I did before. He's more willing to go down on prices and I leave happy
with a couple of glass vases, what I think is a French majolica fish plate,
a wall mirror and some less memorable things. Back at the store, I take*

a better look: the fish plate has "Earl to Mom 1992" scratched into the back. Earl did a real nice job! Too bad the octopus only has five legs left. One of the vases is marked as being French, though, and appears to be something special: Tortoise-shell glass of some sort, quite beautiful. I put a huge price on it and set it in a display case, planning to have it appraised before I actually try to sell it. Lucky for me Darren drops into the store just after I've done that! He takes a look at the tag, of course, and in a moment he's dashing up to the counter with the vase held like a hot-potato.

"I wouldn't have sold it if I knew it was from France!" he wails. "I didn't look on the bottom! I had no idea!" Oh, snap! Stupid me! I have to explain how the plate was crap but I wasn't going to ask for my money back, and that I really don't know what the vase is worth and.... by the time I get done, he's made a small pile of items he wants to buy! Without money... willing to have me come "shop" at his house again for trade. Ohhhh.... Poor guy!

Which all goes to illustrate the perils of clinging to one's goods. Or to loving beautiful things. Or to being human and holding dear what brings you pleasure. I don't blame Darren. I'm only afraid he's going to end up standing on the sidewalk amid a small sea of incredible lamps and Maxfield Parrish prints, shaking a beautiful cloisonne cup for change.

PART III: SAYONARA, OLD STUFF!

CHAPTER 18: THE ELEPHANTS (AND RELATIVES) IN THE ROOM

As this book isn't written to tell you how to make money selling antiques, but rather how to divest yourself of estate items, there are often considerations that will influence your choices, considerations that can't be ignored. The knotty problem of family, for instance. Dealing with siblings, kids, parents (Can you hear me groaning?) while simultaneously navigating a situation of grief or stress is tough! Decisions have to be made and in hindsight they won't all be the best. But to know that going in gives you license to forgive yourself later. Pardon the cliché, but unless the estate is cut and dried; unless you're divesting yourself of the goods of someone you never knew or never cared for, you may be rafting down a tricky river, knuckles white on the paddles as you hang on just trying to keep afloat. You can't worry about doing everything perfectly. If you can make it through the rapids, you will have succeeded in a big way – never mind if your flashlight, your lunch, and a bit of your dignity go overboard.

Other considerations in selling estate items include love, guilt, nostalgia, greed, and need. Just to name a few! Does your need to sell Mom's china outweigh the guilt you feel at doing it? Often we just don't have room for the furniture, dishes, etc., that we feel responsible for. But *they're just things*, I tell myself. And it's likely that mom herself would have parted with them had the need arisen. My own mother was devastatingly *un*sentimental about keeping things, which has made it far easier for me to deaccession stuff I don't have room for. Would Mom want you paying for four storage units in order to hang onto things you can't enjoy? You won't lose your dear one by jettisoning items that have no actual value to you. If possible, choose a few smaller things that have meaning, knowing that Mom would've fully approved of your going on a nice cruise with the proceeds from her sterling flatware. Just because it meant a lot to her, doesn't mean *you* have to feel that way, too. (Some of us – even at our age! – feel that we need permission to take that safari, buy that facelift, or take in a Broadway show for the first time ever: You have my permission! Sell the stuff! Enjoy! Live it up!)

Still, we all know that they're *not* just things. They hold meaning for us: memories, and a way to literally hold onto the past. These are not easy waters to navigate!

Older ladies (yes, it's always women above 60 or so) often tell me about the precious whatnots that they're saving for their children. I always want to suggest that they *ask* the kids if they want those things before spending time and storage space: my guess is that more often than not the kids don't care so much; that what's important to the parents may have little meaning to the younger generation.

Obviously, weighing the pros and cons of any decision can be far more complex than a checklist accounts for. Let's use the example of say, a beautiful French Art Deco necklace in its original box from the 1920s. Your mother inherited it from her mother, who was gifted it by Baron Toucan of York, her filthy-rich old boyfriend. When you and your sister divided the household goods and treasures, you chose this instead of a painting Sister liked. You love it and have fond memories of Mom wearing it. (So does Auntie Charlotte, unfortunately... and she'll never let you forget it!)

It turns out Sister's picture is only worth about $500 while you've had the jewelry appraised at $5,000. She's said, "Oh, don't worry about it ... as long as you don't sell it... just enjoy!" But "enjoying" it now means paying for a safe-deposit box or worrying constantly about theft. And considering that you live like a monk, it's highly unlikely you'll be wearing the necklace anytime soon. On the other hand, it's an heirloom! You *can't* just sell it! If you did, Sister would be mad, Charlotte would blow a cork, and so would... well, Mom wouldn't have wanted you to. Still, the water pump is busted, the Model T needs tires, and the roof is flying away shingle by shingle. You sure could use that $5,000! (On the third hand, with the price of gold going up and up...hmmm... would it be a good investment to just keep it till you're 90?)

Thus, a choice fraught with guilt, need, and the idea that you're responsible to both your mom and sister... and what about Charlotte? There's no way to get through this without regret of some sort. If you sell the jewelry, you'll be giving up a family heirloom, but also the burden of owning it and paying to keep it safe. If you sell it – even assuming you share the proceeds with Sister – you may be angering family members. (Awkward to ask her to buy it, but it may be worth it to her to keep it in the family.) Would a photograph of Mom wearing it really take the place of the object itself? Maybe! In too many instances, there aren't any simple answers. Letting that sleeping dog lie might just work... until you start resenting both Sister and Aunt Charlotte for the guilt they've heaped on you... and because your roof is leaking onto the velvet jewelry box.

Having an expensive necklace to worry about is a luxurious reason to be stressed out, for sure. Even in the context of your own life it's probably an extravagant worry – and one that you don't need. Education is ammunition, meaning look into whether there's a fine-jewelry auction that seems appropriate, get an auction estimate from the auction house, find out if a local jeweler may be interested in purchasing it, or look into consigning it. With the facts in hand your ultimate decision can be more carefully – and logically – made.

It's possible there's a middle-ground solution that'll at least partially satisfy the relatives (and your anxiety level), for instance, selling the necklace and donating part of the proceeds to Mom's favorite charity.

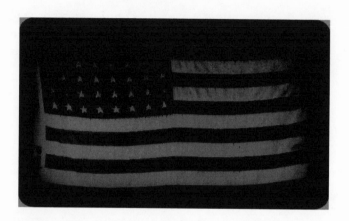

CHAPTER 19: SORTING IT ALL OUT

There are loads of books on how to organize things in an orderly manner – no doubt written by organized people. Of which I am not one! When I need to sort things out to move, find my floor, or just conquer a tabletop heaped with treasures, I follow the old standby of: Keep, Toss, Donate, Sell, and Maybe departments. For your purposes you may also want to add a Give category for things that friends and relatives may want.

If an item in, say, the Donate pile still screams your name after a day or two, switch it to Keep. If a Keep item is already worrying you (where will you store it?, etc.), you might move it to Sell. If guilt descends after piling Dad's Civil War books in Sell, it may ease your mind to donate them to the local Veteran's Administration hospital. In my own experience, leaving loads of give-aways at the Salvation Army or Goodwill has proven to be doubly satisfying, both in the charitable aspect and with the knowledge that those things are gone for good!

Decisions, Decisions! Options! Options!

There may literally be dozens of decisions to be made. Remembering Grandpa Jim while playing his old guitar may well be far more valuable to you than any money. But drunken Uncle Charles's liquor cabinet?

Not so much! Some calls will be obvious. So another sorting job is in order with the things that aren't going to be tossed, shared with relatives, or donated: sell or keep. It's a list that may just sit in your head for days or even years as you debate the pros and cons. I still have items I have to decide what to do with, but it's not costing me anything to hold onto them.

Here are some considerations that may help you when sorting:

- Is the item something you actively enjoy? Do you use it, wear it or have it on display?

- If so, what would you lose or gain by selling it? (IE, by selling the Victrola, you'll lose the ability to play your old 78s – and the memory of Great-Granny dancing to a foxtrot – but you'll gain some money and space in your living room.)

- Is the item something you even *want* to be able to enjoy? (If you've never been fishing and hate the water, why hang onto Aunt Shelly's fishing poles?) If the answer is No, put it aside.

- If you don't presently enjoy it, is it reasonable to envision a future when you'll be able to use it? For instance, if you store the big walnut buffet for a year, will you have room for it in the new house you're building? And if so, is it worth the cost of storing it?)

- If you want to keep it for the future, what's the cost of hanging onto it until you can enjoy it? Money? Mental anguish? Family strife? (IE, if your wife would rather *not* live with your late dad's stuffed moose head hanging over your bed while you plan your fantasy cabin in the woods!) Physical space? Time caretaking? Loss of a profit you might make selling it?

More decisions: Do you sell the stuff in one fell swoop (and possibly at a big loss) and be done with it?, take your time finding just the right way to dispose of each item?, or cling to it all until the universe tells you what to do? Take a deep breath, drink half a glass of Merlot and stare balefully into the fire for half the night. The answer will arrive in a wisp of smoke:

Assuming all your relatives have snagged what they want, there are lots of options. Here are some ideas to play with while the fire dies down and the Merlot wraps your sternum in flannel:

> Rent storage units to keep everything. This may give you time to think over your options and to let the dust settle.

> Hold a garage sale for the lower-value items. You don't want to advertise that your house is chockful of Tiffany lamps and sterling candlesticks by arraying them along your driveway, right?, so the schlockier the better. Garage-salers love crap. They love to drag it home to their own garages. America's all about it: *the more crap the better*. To paraphrase George Carlin, they don't call it "stuff" fr nuthin! You can stuff your crap into nooks and crannys, the car trunk, your kid's doll's trunk, the empty backyard pool… why do you think rich people have cabanas? What do you think is *in* those cabanas, anyway? Rich crap that they bought at rich peoples' garage sales (also known politely as "charity events").

> Send special items or groups of items to local auction, for instance all the better glass, Dad's collectible trains, Aunt Duckie's linens and silver, the grandfather clock

> Sell the car on Craigslist

> Consign the Degas to a high-end auction house

> Talk with an estate services company about buying all the contents that are left

> Give some or all to charity

CHAPTER 20: GETTING UNSTUCK

Should you be either downsizing your own estate or helping a relative move – especially an older relative or friend who isn't happy about moving – taking photographs of every room of the house prior to moving items may be a comfort later on. Don't forget to take photos of, say, mom's photo wall, her beloved piano laid with sheet music, even her open kitchen cupboards and stove. Leaving things behind is difficult enough, but at least the memories of those good times and family mementos can be kept in an album and shared together.

If Mom's wedding day was the happiest she ever had, it may be smart to keep and frame the veil for her. Likewise if your late father's stamp collection is evocative of good times you had together, keep a page under the glass of your coffee table or color copy it before selling.

When downsizing it's easy to get stuck on the idea that sets of things need to stay together. For instance, the mother you're helping to move into a retirement home may love the sterling flatware she got as a wedding gift some 60 years ago. In her small new kitchen, though, there won't be room to house the entire set; neither will she have any need for a dozen place settings and serving pieces… plus, it just wouldn't be safe to keep it there, as aides and housekeepers will be visiting frequently. Mom might be initially aghast at the suggestion that she break up the set and keep just four place settings for herself… but why not? If you don't plan to keep the remainder yourself, it can be sold as is… and no one will ever complain that it's missing four settings!

The same holds true for, say, a dining room ensemble of table, buffe and china hutch. Of course the dining room holds so many grea memories of holidays, parties and family. Your mom may balk a breaking up "the set" that's graced her home for so many years, but i you can get her to worry less about what she's leaving behind and focus more on what she'll be keeping and enjoying, she can continue to fine happiness in, say, the china hutch alone. Should the rest be sold, no one will wonder where the hutch is; they'll simply be happy with what they've purchased.

Once Mom begins to see that she doesn't have to give up entire sets of her special things, she may find some fun in figuring out how to save samples of treasured items. My father, for instance, was given an antique chess set from a friend who, as a child, I looked up to. By the time the house had to be cleaned out, some 40 years later, a number of the pieces were broken or missing, but neither Dad nor I wanted the rest to be disposed of. We both saved several chess men, and now that he's gone, too, I'm gratified to have them.

Favorite sets that Mom might sample could include books, dishes, a piece of a collection rather than the whole thing. While it may pain her to keep only one of the Victorian pitchers out of the dozens that she owns, a photo album of the rest will preserve those, too.

If she wants to keep her late husband's old wrench from his tool box or the side mirror off his truck you're donating, more power to her! Mementos come in all sorts of forms.

Best Wishes!

It's hoped that by now you have a better idea of what to do with estate items of all sorts. Feel free to email suggestions, corrections, and ideas for the next edition!

QUICK RULES OF THUMB

1. There is no absolute value for anything. "What's it worth?" only means "What can I get for it under these circumstances?" The market sets the value, not the other way around.

2. It always costs time or money or both to sell something. How much is it worth to you to have Aunt Frieda's ugly lamp gone?

3. Knowledge is truly power when it comes to selling an older item: the more you know about its general value, its history, what it is and what it isn't, the smarter a seller you can be.

4. The more you know about your options in selling something, the better a choice you'll make.

5. You can buy a certain degree of knowledge in hiring an appraiser… but it will take some knowledge on your part to estimate whether the cost will be worth it!

6. If it was schlock when it was new, it probably hasn't gained in value.

7. If it was made to be collectible, it's not.

8. Just because it's old doesn't mean it's valuable.

9. Ballsy assertion does not equal knowledge. Don't be blinded by baloney!

10. There are no wrong decisions; only more or less informed ones.

11. Don't look back!

Made in the USA
San Bernardino, CA
26 February 2014